Michel Tournier

La Goutte d'or

Michael Worton

Professor of French,
University College, London.

UNIVERSITY of GLASGOW
FRENCH AND GERMAN PUBLICATIONS
1995

University of Glasgow French and German Publications

Series Editors: Mark G. Ward (German)
Geoff Woollen (French)

Consultant Editors: Colin Smethurst
Kenneth Varty

Modern Languages Building, University of Glasgow,
Glasgow G12 8QL, Scotland.

First published 1992; reprinted 1995.

Printed by BPC Wheatons Ltd., Exeter.

ISBN 0 85261 270 2

Contents

Acknowledgments

I must first of all thank Michel Tournier for giving me access both to the manuscript of *La Goutte d'or* and to his working notebooks—and also for the many discussions over the fifteen years of our friendship which have aided me enormously in preparing this book.

Many of my ideas have been discussed with other Tournier specialists. I thank them all for their useful comments, but I should like to express special gratitude to Kirsty Fergusson, Françoise Merllié, Mireille Rosello and the late Lynn Salkin Sbiroli for their perceptive insights. I would also like to thank Lawrence E. Klein for his attentive reading of the manuscript and for all his helpful advice on the organisation of my arguments, and Geoff Woollen, for editing my text and compiling the Glossary.

Some of the original work on this book was done in France on a grant from the British Academy, to whom I extend my thanks.

Michael Worton   London, April 1992

Introduction

On a first reading, *La Goutte d'or* appears to be a straightforward text. It tells a story which, while specifically about a young North African's voyage of self-discovery, has universal implications in that each of us can identify with many of Idriss's adventures, albeit in a personal and refracted way. Tournier here treats several of his abiding concerns, such as initiation, travel, the relationship between the individual and society, reading, etymology, intertextuality, and the place and function of images and documentation in contemporary society. So why was it controversial?

To an extent, the controversy concerned its apparent involvement in political debate about immigration, yet it also centred on what 'should' be the relationship between fact and fiction, between documentation and imagination in a novel. The fact is that the novel is much more than a political novel. The controversy reflected this, since, when the novel was not seen as documentary, it was seen as even more subversive and anti-European. Always provocative, Tournier launches, in *La Goutte d'or*, his most explicit assault on European political and aesthetic attitudes and on what he perceives as the smugness of Eurocentric thinking—whilst also studding his text with references and allusions to French literature and songs!

His aggressive position explains in part the hostile reaction of several French critics who felt either that he was 'betraying' France and the French literary tradition or that the novel was too simple, a mere exploitation of documentary sources. However, this novel has a complexity which is still not fully recognised: there are many fewer articles or chapters devoted to it than to any of Tournier's other novels. The obvious explanation would be that it is a fairly recent text and that critics are still mulling over their responses to it; however, *Le Médianoche amoureux* (1989) has already attracted many more pages of serious criticism, so one cannot but suspect that there is some wilfulness—or some blindness—in the reluctance of critics to engage with *La Goutte d'or*. This critical blindness worries me, because I feel that *La Goutte d'or* is both one of Tournier's most important novels and one of his most readable.

In the 1990s, when all European parliaments are debating the issue of immigration even more urgently and violently than in 1985, *La Goutte d'or* offers a salutary reminder that we need to take a real account of otherness. My own experience of teaching this novel has revealed that readers are both shocked and fascinated by it: shocked into a re-evaluation of Eurocentric positions, and fascinated by the novel's play with literature and philosophy. All Tournier's previous novels challenge readers to read beyond his text and to enter the labyrinth of cultural history, but *La Goutte d'or* does this in an exciting way, asking readers to pose themselves new questions about their position and function as readers.

While the novel is undoubtedly political, it also poses a series of philosophical questions about what a novel can and should be. Tournier has repeatedly recognised his intellectual debt to Sartrean theories of existentialism, but he diverges from Sartre in his insistence on the reader's co-creativity: for Tournier, all intellectual activity is a game, but a game which can have serious consequences.

So, how to read and interpret *La Goutte d'or?* I had initially intended to include some maps of Paris and the Sahar and images of Arabic calligraphy, but I finally decided to exclude such 'aids'. This decision arose from my belief that one of the aims of the novel is to make us think about what a novel is and can do, and that another aim is to remind us that ignorance is not a terminal state. In Tournier's view, a novel is a source of information and instruction; it is also, as he argues in the introduction to his collection of literary essays *Le Vol du vampire,* a vampire which both preys on readers and depends for its existence on their various reactions:

> Un livre n'a pas un auteur, mais un nombre indéfini d'auteurs. [...] Un livre écrit, mais non lu, n'existe pas pleinement. Il ne possède qu'une demi-existence. C'est une virtualité, un être exsangue, vide, malheureux qui s'épuise dans un appel à l'aide pour exister. (*VV,* 12)

Above all, the novel demands that we think for ourselves and make our own decisions about how important some word or plot detail is. Much of the pleasure of reading *La Goutte d'or* comes from having to reconsider and recontextualise an apparently standard image and from having to look up unfamiliar words—which can subsequently become part of our individual lexicons.

While the plot of *La Goutte d'or* is simple and has a reassuring narrative logic, the novel is also pleasingly complex in its presentation of Idriss's voyage of self-discovery. As readers, we not only follow the progress of the young protagonist, but find ourselves caught up in a web of intercultural and intertextual speculation. Therefore, my study seeks to point up the novel's ludic play with a variety of ideas and sources. The temptation to give a chronological or linear reading had to be resisted, for the novel itself contests the logic of linearity, constantly referring backwards and forwards within itself and referring 'outside' to other texts (several of them Tournier's own works). For this reason, I felt it useful to focus on what I see as the main themes of *La Goutte d'or,* and to organise my book in a way which would foreground Tournier's art.

La Goutte d'or is a radically modern novel. A kaleidoscopic text, it poses more questions than it gives answers, yet perhaps the questions are themselves already most of the answers. In other words, my book seeks to mime the simplicity and complexity of Tournier's novel—in the hope and expectation that other readers will complete my work.

Chapter One

Politics and beyond

Michel Tournier is no stranger to controversy. All of his novels have provoked extreme reactions, be these of admiration or anger. He is probably still best known for *Le Roi des aulnes,* which Janet Flanner described in *The New Yorker* as 'the most important book to come out in France since Proust' and which such eminent thinkers as Susan Sontag and George Steiner acclaimed as one of the few really important European novels of the postwar period. Yet this novel also offends many people who see in it an apology for Nazism. Tournier's response is best expressed in the *Newsweek* interview-article 'A Writer Rages' (6 November 1989): 'When people tell me I estheticize Nazism, I quote Léon Blum who said "communism is a technique, socialism a morality, and fascism an esthetic"'. As so often, Tournier was speaking tongue in cheek, but his underlying point is serious and firmly believed. For him, political ideologies are above all *systems*—which writers have the right and, indeed, the duty to expose as the shameless (and, he would add, the shameful) constructs they are.

It is this *textual* quality of political systems that Tournier repeatedly exploits and attacks in his work, reminding us of the artificiality of most ideological positions—although he himself has several strongly-held beliefs, notably on the position of immigrant workers in Western Europe and on abortion. In the controversial *Newsweek* article, he said:

> Abortionists are the sons and grandsons of the monsters of Auschwitz. Even worse are husbands or lovers who force women to get abortions because the men don't want children. I would reinstate the death penalty for such people.

Predictably, he was (venomously) attacked by both Right and Left, by both pro-life and pro-choice campaigners, mainly because of his choice of vocabulary. However, his critics were blind to the *rhetorical* nature of his statement. For Tournier, rhetoric is the domain of those who know how to use and manipulate language. Hyperbole is, after all, a *trope* or figure of speech and should be read and received as such— especially when it is used in the context of an interview. While it is certain that Tournier is committedly 'pro-life', all of his statements on 'the family', be they written or oral, need to be read in the context of his concept of the writer as an essentially subversive being, as the (correctively) corrupting worm within the apple.

Tournier is perhaps unique amongst contemporary French writers in that he is claimed and reviled by both Right and Left. This paradox is illuminating, for it reveals the chasm that separates political discourse from literary discourse. Tournier repeatedly insists on his own marginal position as a French writer who despises French chauvinism and, regarding Paris, speaks of 'mon antipathie radicale envers ma ville natale' (*VP*, 21). However, in every book or article he publishes and in virtually every conversation, he alludes to a multiplicity of French authors, often quoting at length—and accurately—from memory. He provocatively asserts that writers have 'un degré de "francité" incomparable', in that they have 'des relations constantes, intimes, orageuses, amoureuses, bref conjugales' (*VP*, 88) with the French language. His comment on Brasillach is characteristic of his position:

> Le réquisitoire qui entraîna la condamnation à mort et l'exécution de Robert Brasillach—écrivain médiocre et traître majeur au demeurant—ne fut qu'une sinistre cacologie vomie par un ramassis de métèques mal débarbouillés. Moi, écrivain français, j'ai le privilège de par ma francité supérieure de pouvoir si bon me semble accabler la France des pires critiques, des injures les plus sales, vous qui me lisez, si vous n'êtes pas vous-même écrivain français, je vous accorde tout juste le droit de m'écouter debout et découvert, comme si vous entendiez *La Marseillaise*. (*VP*, 88)

It is clear that Tournier has no sympathy for Brasillach's political affiliations and little admiration for his literary worth, yet in a footnote added in 1979 to the Folio edition of *Le Vent Paraclet* he offers an alternative expression of his argument, stating that Brasillach's judges 'écrivaient le français moins bien que lui, bien qu'il ne fût pas—tant s'en faut—un écrivain de premier ordre' (*VP*, 308). This privileging of writers shocks many people who do not recognise Tournier's provocative sense of humour, yet the point is also meant seriously. Because of their intimate relationship with language, writers can engage more forcefully in political debates. Tournier himself is in many ways an establishment figure (a member of the Académie Goncourt and courted by many politicians, notably President Mitterrand), but he uses this power to subvert the system from within. A key to his position is the notion of transgression. While he was undoubtedly upset by the many attacks made on him after the *Newsweek* article, he also revelled in the fact that a writer could cause such seismic reactions by articulating personal beliefs in socially transgressive terms.

This footnote in *Le Vent Paraclet* reveals his determination to use all terms in the lexicon—provided that they are used properly:

> j'affectionne tout particulièrement le mot *métèque*, l'un des derniers 'gros mots' qui nous restent, et peut-être le dernier. Lorsqu'il aura disparu—ou, ce qui revient au même, quand sa force d'invective se sera éventée—il ne nous restera plus aucun moyen de transgression verbale. (*VP*, 308)

There is a problem, of course, since most people, and especially politicians, use language sloppily. This both angers and amuses Tournier, who takes pleasure in discovering in books or media reports such logically impossible phrases as 'saupoudrer de sel' or 'une déstabilisation de la révolution'. However, his insistence on linguistic precision in his own discourse is no guarantee that he will not be misunderstood. For example, in a public lecture in Rio de Janeiro in 1987, he gave an analysis of contemporary France in which he used an extended metaphor: 'la France est comme une bouse de vache'. Politicians such as Mitterrand, Giscard d'Estaing and Rocard were compared to flies walking on the dried crust of a cow-pat, unaware of what is happening in the organic ferment beneath them. The image was both thought through and meant seriously—as a metaphor. As such, it works well and amusingly, as long as one recognizes that this is a rhetorical ploy. Alas, when it was reported in the Brazilian newspapers, a journalist translated the image as if he had said that 'la France est un tas de merde', with the result that the French Ambassador felt that Tournier had insulted France! He used the image again in the 1989 *Newsweek* interview, where the 'bouse de vache' was (badly) translated as 'a pile of cow dung'. These mistranslations upset Tournier, yet he also takes pleasure in noting how dangerous it is to use language creatively when few people respect (or are even aware of) the specificity of individual words or images.

His various researches for *La Goutte d'or* convinced him that France was becoming increasingly racist, that racism was going to be appropriated as a political plank by all parties, and that political rhetoric would become increasingly manipulative—and bankrupt. This has recently been proved by the fact that the Socialist president François Mitterrand spoke in 1990 of the 'seuil de tolérance' being crossed, an image taken up by the new President Jacques Chirac in speeches in 1991 which went even further, using images of greedy, smelly, noisy immigrants in his offensive against France's coloured population. Furthermore, when in 1991 Valéry Giscard d'Estaing made remarks about 'une invasion d'immigrés', thereby cynically exploiting a word which has painful connotations for the French, his words brought him an immediate dividend: opinion polls immediately showed him to be the politician with whom most of the French identify! These are blatant attempts to seize votes from Jean-Marie Le Pen's Front National by playing up to primitive racist responses. Yet they are 'justified' by politicians of both the Left and the Centre-Right who use the tactical argument that if tough immigration controls, forced repatriation and camps for asylum seekers are not introduced, then fascism will once again sweep through Europe. This argument is, of course, fatally flawed and indeed it was counterpointed or countermanded by the publication in 1991 of reports by the O.E.C.D. and by I.N.S.E.E. (the French official statistics office), both of which pointed out that France will soon need more immigrant workers to make up for its falling birth rate. And yet politicians from all parties continue to advocate the expulsion of jobless foreigners, the re-establishment of strict identity checks, and an end to the automatic right of citizenship by birth.

This so-called 'political realism' is nothing other than appeasement. It capitulates before the assumed racism of the white European voter and ignores the fact that racial attitudes, which are an unstable mix of fears and fantasies, can in fact be changed both through education and through legislation. Throughout Europe, but most flagrantly in France, politicians are capitulating before what they see as a rising tide of xenophobia rather than attempting to lead and shape public opinion. In this they are aided and abetted by the press and even, scandalously, sometimes by the Church. For instance, in September 1991, *Le Méridional,* the local daily newspaper of Marseille, where North Africans are in the vast majority in many districts, recalled the words of the late Houari Boumedienne, the Algerian nationalist leader: 'No atomic bomb will stop our peoples one day invading the rich spaces of the northern hemisphere'. This was scaremongering at its most sophisticated, in that Boumedienne's statement, albeit inflammatory, was not intended to equate North Africans with the Nazi forces which invaded France in the Second World War—but the French press and Giscard could seize upon and distort his use of one word. Furthermore, while the bishops and archbishops of France continue to condemn racism, many parish priests ignore their lead and quote with approbation the sentiments expressed in 1990 by Monsignor Ersilio Tonnini, the Archbishop of Ravenna, who complained that Europe was being Islamicised and that peoples of different cultures, religions and races could not live in harmony together.

Despite his constant stance as a severe critic of France and its social, legal and fiscal codes, Tournier is deeply committed to French culture and is evidently seduced by the paradoxes of French life. For example, he enjoys pointing out how and why French politicians feel the need to define themselves as 'littéraires'—in order to please voters who still accord great importance to writers and intellectuals. He is fond of reminding us that when Bernard Pivot invited politicians to speak on his television book-programme *Apostrophes* about their reading habits, Raymond Barre (then Prime Minister) badly misquoted the first line of his 'favourite poem', Valéry's 'Le Cimetière marin' (showing a disregard for the laws of scansion), and François Léotard (then Minister of Culture!) cited as his regular and essential bedside reading Flaubert's (non-existent) *Journal*. These errors were, for Tournier, symptomatic of the way in which French politicians refer crudely and manipulatively to literature in an attempt to win votes and consequently risk exposing their own ignorance. However, the very fact that a literary background is viewed as a vote-catcher reinforces Tournier's belief that literature continues to matter in France, not as an ornament but as a central element in the ongoing process of the establishment of national identity.

The writer is perhaps the last legitimate(d) terrorist in France, and Tournier determinedly exploits the freedom granted to writers. *Vendredi ou les limbes du Pacifique* (1967), for example, was read by ethnologists as a novel about ethnocide, by hippies as a programme for a return to Nature and, by some critics in the U.S.A. as a eulogy for Black power. *Les Météores* (1975) was both hailed as an important intervention in debates on sexuality and identity and reviled as a 'plaidoyer' for homosexuality; *Gilles & Jeanne* (1983) was admired and attacked for its speculative rewriting of the legends of Joan of Arc and 'Bluebeard', Gilles de Rais; and *Gaspard, Melchior et Balthazar* (1980) was welcomed by some bishops and priests as a deeply theological novel and attacked by others as a heretical text. (The most perceptive theological remark on Tournier's Christian position was perhaps made by his former confessor, Monsignor Georges Assemaine, a priest-teacher at the St. Erembert school where he studied from 1935-1938, who, after reading the manuscript, said to the author: 'Je ne sais pas si vous avez la Foi, mais vous avez la Grâce').

Even his most ardent admirers may, however, occasionally be alienated by such extravagant statements as his commentary on the brutal tonsillotomy which traumatized him at the age of four years (and thereby provided him with an image of blood-letting that haunts almost all his novels):

> quarante-cinq ans plus tard, j'en porte encore les traces et je reste incapable d'évoquer cette scène de sang-froid. Au cours de la dernière guerre des fillettes impubères furent violées par la soldatesque. J'affirme qu'elles en furent moins traumatisées qu'un enfant de quatre ans après une pareille scène d'égorgement... (*VP*, 18)

It is certain that Tournier enjoys shocking his readers, but his intention goes beyond a desire to 'épater le bourgeois'. He seeks to force our attention onto areas of personal and social existence that we prefer to leave in the shadows. We may deplore some of the hyperbolic writing, yet cannot but recognise that its shock value invites us to challenge received notions and demands a personal (and frequently disquieting) engagement both with his texts and with our own psychic histories.

9

In the years between the publication of his 'intellectual autobiography' *Le Vent Paraclet* (1977) and his major collection of literary essays, *Le Vol du vampire* (1981), Tournier read a lot of critical theory and changed his attitude towards the reader. He moved from a position of willed authority to a recognition of the co-creative role of readers in the (never-ending) establishment of a text's textuality. However, it is important to note that Tournier's concept of the reader is determined in great part by his own childhood and adult experiences: many of his more recent texts insist on reading as valid only if it is passionate, and in his frequent talks to schoolchildren he urges them to learn to find authors they love, even if they can't fully articulate why they love them. This may seem strange on the part of a writer who is so devoted to philosophy and to linguistic precision, but over the past thirty years Tournier has been a professional reader, first as a broadcaster and as a translator from German into French, then as a member of the *comité de lecture* of Éditions Gallimard, and as a regular reviewer in newspapers and magazines. Since 1967, he has also annually received hundreds of letters from 'naïve' readers, each of which he treasures and responds to. Consequently he has come to a belief that 'Le lecteur amateur [...] est un vrai lecteur, le seul qui compte profondément', whereas the critic or professional reader is a form of prostitute who must have 'un *devoir de duplicité*'. [1]

The paradox of Tournier's position as 'amateur' and 'professional' reader and as writer finds its fullest fictional articulation in *Le Médianoche amoureux,* which is neither really a novel nor merely a collection of short stories. In form, it is deliberately modelled on Boccacio's *Decamerone* and Marguerite de Navarre's *Heptaméron,* but a more crucial intertext is *The Arabian Nights,* in which Scheherazade tells her husband a story every night in order to save or at least prolong her life. In Tournier's text, writing and reading (in the form of telling and listening to stories) are posited as the means to save a marriage. Yet even here Tournier consciously subverts his own project by insisting on the recuperative powers of the *conte,* or fairy tale, and on the destructive powers of the *nouvelle,* or realist short story. And this distinction is established by a writer who repeatedly proclaims his allegiance to nineteenth-century French realism!

Each of his texts is rich in discursive challenges to received values— and each undermines its own apparent authority from within. This was immediately perceived by an unlikely promoter for Tournier's work, Raymond Queneau, who, as reader for Gallimard and as member of the Académie Goncourt, admired in *Vendredi:*

la richesse d'idées et d'inventions de ce récit, richesse, il faut bien le dire,

[1] Michel Tournier, 'Quand Raymond Queneau "lisait" Tournier', *Sud,* XVIe année, 61 (1986), 7-8.

parfois un peu sophistiquée et même frelatée. [C'est] un livre bien curieux dont la publication me paraît s'imposer.

Queneau later identified in *Le Roi des aulnes:*

> une ambition démesurée, bourrée d'allusions et d'allégories, moins profonde qu'elle ne veut être et qui serait plus convaincante si 'l'ogre' ne montait pas sur scène pour parler de son 'moi' au public, le moi de quelqu'un qui a lu Bataille, Klossoswski [*sic*], etc. [2]

Tournier chose to publish Queneau's remarks in order to demonstrate how professional readers can and must champion works which they may personally dislike, even detest, when these have genuine literary or intellectual merit. It is, though, undeniable that Tournier is much more interested in the responses of amateur readers than in the comments of literary critics or scholars, however flattering these may be.

He is determined to intervene in political and moral debates, often insisting that writers should seek influence but not power, influence being a form of moral persuasion, not coercion. Yet he also seeks to 'tell good stories' and to write so simply and so clearly that ten-year-old children can read him: *Vendredi,* rewritten for children as *Vendredi ou la vie sauvage* (1971), is annually studied in hundreds of French schools and has sold more than two and a half million copies.

This paradox is evident in *La Goutte d'or,* which juxtaposes a limpid style with a rich and often erudite vocabulary—and which marries a philosophico-anthropological meditation on the difference between the purity of the Islamic sign and the corruptive force of the Western (Christian) image with an assault on recent Western, and especially French, political attitudes towards immigration.

Tournier has many admirers amongst reviewers, but also many enemies. Both camps had a field day when *La Goutte d'or* appeared in 1985, in the run-up to the French parliamentary elections. It was an explosive time to publish a novel about a young Saharan shepherd immigrating to France. Jean-Marie Le Pen was calling for the compulsory repatriation of immigrants—and racism was becoming a politically acceptable position! Everyone seemed to have forgotten that in the 1950s the same Le Pen had insisted that France was not just the 'hexagon' but also the D.O.M. and T.O.M. ('domaines d'outre-mer' and 'territoires d'outre-mer'), and that the French 'empire' should be preserved at all costs. The debates were even more fierce than those following Enoch Powell's 1969 'rivers of blood' speech in Britain, so when an established—and establishment—writer published a novel which was (partially) about the problems encountered by an immigrant, the reactions of the media were violent. Tournier was accused of opportunism (although he had been working on the novel for several

---

[2] 'Quand Raymond Queneau "lisait" Tournier', pp. 9-10.

years), of anti-patriotism, and even of treason.

On the other hand, his explicit novelistic intervention into the political arena was hailed, notably by the Left, as a belated proof of commitment, of Sartrean *engagement*. All of these responses were, however, blind to the textual evidence of Tournier's committed interest in ethnic 'minorities' from 1967 onwards. Furthermore, it should be stressed that he was much marked by his ethnological studies with Claude Lévi-Strauss at the Musée de l'Homme, as is testified by his essay in *Le Vol du vampire* (pp. 397-400). Confronted initially—and then fascinated—by the *otherness* of foreign cultures through his study of ethnology, he soon began to perceive connections with the otherness which France imposes on its own marginal groups, be they immigrants, sexual or religious minorities, the blind or deaf, or whatever, and long before he became a published novelist he drew attention to the societal problem of minorities in some of his broadcasts. One of Lévi-Strauss's most fertile and provocative ideas is that each culture feeds off other cultures but must also have some *resistance* to them, otherwise it will have nothing to exchange. This idea is grounded in the North American Indian custom of potlatch, which consisted in the extravagant giving of presents to enemy tribe leaders as a form of generous challenge.

The cultural resonances of the potlatch have inspired much modern French thought from Bataille and Lévi-Strauss to Lacan, all of whom Tournier has read. It is therefore not surprising that in all his work he combines an ethnological concern with otherness with a writerly preoccupation with exchange (this latter point is examined at greater length in Chapter Four).

Tournier's interest in the question of ethnic difference is patent especially in *Vendredi*, but also in *Gaspard, Melchior et Balthazar*, in which he meditates, from a Western European and anti-historical, if Biblically consonant position, on the problematic difference between image and resemblance and on the negative self-images which Judeo-Christian culture has imposed on Blacks. Gaspard opens with the sentence, 'Je suis noir, mais je suis roi' (*GMB*, 9). The text immediately exposes itself as a paraphrase of the celebrated *Nigra sum, sed formosa* in the *Song of Solomon* (I: 5), and in many ways the novel is an exploration of the ideological, philosophical and aesthetic implications of the *mais*, the *sed*, the *but*. In other words, Tournier is concerned not so much with *négritude* as with *between-ness* and the question of why and how we are made to feel the need to justify ourselves against prevailing ideologies.

The same preoccupation haunts *Les Météores*, which anatomizes heterosexuality, the 'love that need not speak its name', from the perspective of a promiscuously cruising gay man, Alexandre Surin. It also haunts *Gilles & Jeanne*, where sanctity and depravity are posited as states of desire, of simultaneous uncertainty and quest. The most powerful textual presentation of Tournier's anxious awareness of liberal European Caucasian responses to the 'Third World' is, perhaps, to be found in *Le Vent Paraclet*, where he explains why he finally abandoned his initial desire to dedicate *Vendredi* to France's immigrant workers:

> le dédicataire me paraissait trop grand, trop respectable, trop éloigné de moi, et je n'avais pas le moyen de lui demander la permission de lui rendre ce dérisoire hommage. Oui, j'aurais voulu dédier ce livre à la masse énorme et silencieuse des travailleurs immigrés de France, tous ces Vendredi dépêchés vers nous par le tiers monde, ces trois millions d'Algériens, de Marocains, de Tunisiens, de Sénégalais, de Portugais sur lesquels repose notre société et qu'on ne voit jamais, qu'on n'entend jamais, qui n'ont ni bulletin de vote, ni syndicat, ni porte-parole. [...] Notre société de consommation est assise sur eux, elle a posé ses fesses grasses et blanches sur ce peuple basané réduit au plus absolu silence. [...] Cette population bâillonnée mais vitale, tolérée mais indispensable, c'est le seul vrai prolétariat qui existe en France. Prenons garde que la voix de cette foule muette n'éclate pas tout à coup à nos oreilles avec un bruit de tonnerre! (*VP*, 236-7)

La Goutte d'or is not a political tract but a novel, and should be read as such. Although its impact resonated well beyond the literary ghettoes, Tournier himself insisted in 1986 that: 'Ce n'est pas un pamphlet, mais c'est contre le racisme et la montée de l'intolérance'.[3] More recently, he has stated that literature is the 'contre-poison du pouvoir politique', whilst also recognising that few writers have changed political systems by their writing.[4] One of his favourite texts is *The Arabian Nights,* whose influence is to be found in the two *contes* in *La Goutte d'or* and in many of the stories in *Le Médianoche amoureux.* He admires Scheherazade's ability to 'désarmer le tyran' in *The Arabian Nights* by telling stories, yet admiration is tempered by the acute realisation that this is a fiction, and by his belief that in reality writers must 'conquérir par conviction et séduction', not by mounting political platforms.[5]

When the critics paid attention to the literary qualities of the novel, it was often to attack his use of documentation, his 'lack of sensitivity and imagination', or to challenge his use of unusual words (many of which have an origin in Arabic culture). In other words, professional readers in 1985 saw the novel not as a novel but as a document— thereby proving Tournier's belief that critics are all too often the slaves of the dominant political ideology! In *La Goutte d'or,* we can undoubtedly find an acerbic assault on French attitudes to immigrant workers. But we must also read it as a novel, as a work of fiction which proclaims its own fictivity in order to exert a more lasting effect on its readers.

[3] See Ezzedine Mestiri, 'En parlant de *La Goutte d'or* avec Michel Tournier', *Hommes et Migrations,* no. 1091 (15 avril 1986), p. 61.

[4] Michel Tournier, 'Le Conteur et la Politique', *Le Croquant,* no. 6, p. 106.

[5] *Ibid.,* pp. 105-106.

Chapter Two

Image and sign

For several years, *La Goutte d'or* was a 'projet de tiroir' on which Tournier worked occasionally while seriously researching a novel about Saint Sebastian. However, in the early 1980s, two events served to focus his attention on the Sahara. First, an architect friend, Pascal Maréchaux, who was then working in the Yemen, arranged to meet Tournier at Béchar in the spring of 1981. Tournier arrived by plane, Maréchaux on his motorbike, and they set off for the southern Sahara with Tournier riding pillion, garlanded by eight petrol cans! Since the road had often disappeared under sand, Tournier would act as lookout for where it might be, while Maréchaux concentrated on keeping the bike upright. They could not visit Tabelbala, since it was considered dangerous because of its proximity to the border with Morocco, then riven by internal strife which amounted almost to a civil war, so they explored the south and then drove up to Ghardaïa in the M'Zab (see **80**)—where Tournier caught a plane while Maréchaux continued on his bike to the Yemen! Second, in 1982, the (formerly Communist) television director Marcel Bluwal asked him to write a screenplay. *La Goutte d'or* was hauled out of its folder, the novel *Saint Sébastien* was temporarily abandoned, though Tournier continued to meditate on the legend of the martyr saint (and is now finally writing that novel), and he immersed himself in immigrant culture as completely as Idriss is forced to do in the vat of alginate which will make of his body a shop-window mannequin. He read voraciously, met with many immigrant workers' groups and even spent a night in a Paris police van, silently noting the responses of the police as they picked up (and picked on) North Africans. After writing the screenplay, he immediately began work on a novelistic version and showed little interest in the fate of the screenplay—which, because of funding problems, was not made into a television film until 1988. (Through a coincidence not of Tournier's making, Idriss was played by the young Moroccan actor Lilah Dadi, who two years earlier had played Vendredi in the stage adaptation of Tournier's first novel at the Théâtre de la Renaissance in Brussels.) His earlier novel *Gilles & Jeanne* also has its origins in a film script—which was written for the director and actor, Gérard Blain. This film has not yet been made (again for funding reasons), but what is important is that

both novels had their genesis in a desire to create visual images. Having
established a plot skeleton and a series of dialogues and visually
interesting scenes, Tournier then chose to forget the originating filmic
project and to work more on the textual elements of his stories.

While Tournier's novel is the story of one young Berber immigrant,
it functions also as an interrogation of the post-colonial French attitude
to North Africa and especially to Algeria. Mustapha, the Béchar
photographer-for-tourists, insists to his French clients that he is a
creative professional who can recreate the Sahara in his studio and
thereby recreate them—because he is there to 'réaliser vos rêves' (**83**).
In 1977, before *La Goutte d'or* was a precise novelistic project,
Tournier arranged to meet his American photographer friend Arthur
Tress in Tangiers, in order to explore Morocco. And in Marrakech,
they came across a photographer who challenged the notion of
photography as revelation-discovery and who was to be the model for
Mustapha:

> Je voyais le visage de Tress se fermer devant tout ce *pittoresque* offert, cet
> étalage trop facile de laideurs sublimes et de beautés grimaçantes, et je
> savais que quelque chose allait nécessairement se produire pour que se
> nouât le charme. Ce fut sous les espèces d'un «confrère» photographe que
> le miracle eut lieu. Mais quel photographe! La façade de sa boutique affectait
> l'aspect d'une cage à fauves. Sa spécialité: le portrait-rêve. Quand un client
> se présente, il commence par le soumettre à une psychanalyse de sa façon.
> Puis il se met au travail Il peint un décor en trompe-l'œil, il rassemble des
> accessoires, il fournit au client un costume, lui barbouille un maquillage.
> ('Mon génial ami Arthur Tress, *CM*, 117-19)

The reader of *La Goutte d'or* initially interprets Mustapha's
photographic practice as a mere example of commercial exploitation,
but, as so often in Tournier's work, a subsequent episode comments on
an earlier event and repositions the reader's response. Philippe, Idriss's
companion in the train to Paris, reveals that he always travels with 'un
tas de photos' as a kind of emotional insurance policy (so his position is
not unlike that of Uncle Mogadem). However, he also asserts: 'Chaque
Français a son idée sur l'Algérie et le Sahara, même s'il n'y a jamais mis
les pieds. Ça fait partie de nos rêves' (**115**). In other words, North
Africa is problematically double for the French, as much of Black
Africa, India and the Caribbean is double for the British: a site of post-
imperialist anxiety and, simultaneously, a target for unresolved cultural
fantasies. This paradox is made most explicit in the novel when the
régisseur (studio manager and property buyer) asks Mage what to do
with the camel they bought for the television commercial for the fruit
juice *Palmeraie*. He reveals that they couldn't hire it but had to buy it
from a circus owner. '—Alors, *s'effare* Mage, le propriétaire, c'est
nous?' Mage, the paying lover of Arab rent-boys, is confronted by the

European 'problem' of North African immigrants. The prop man's
'impitoyable' reply is that of many liberal politicians: 'Exactement [...],
c'est votre chameau. Qu'est-ce qu'on en fait?' (**151**). Mage has no
pragmatic response, but his assistant does:

> —En somme [...], c'est comme les travailleurs immigrés. On croyait les
> avoir loués et pouvoir les renvoyer chez eux quand on n'en aurait plus
> besoin, et puis on s'aperçoit qu'on les a achetés et qu'on doit les garder en
> France. (*ibid.*)

Mage's swerving reaction to this statement is narratively performative.
He engages in a speculation on what a camel is—a speculation which is
deliberately presented as lexically and etymologically suspect, since no
one knows of what they are speaking, and they refer to the script in
order to justify their lack of empirical knowledge (**152**). This serves as
a paradigm for Western European political reactions to inter-racial
problems: a scrutiny of individual words, often taken out of context,
permits politicians to avoid attention to the real issues.

La Goutte d'or presents an anatomisation of French attitudes towards
immigrants from a culture of which Europeans are largely ignorant.
Part of its political thrust comes from its play with words and
metaphors, but the main argument is grounded in its articulation of the
tension between two world-views.

Each of Tournier's novels is structured on and by a binary
opposition which is simultaneously maintained and subverted. In *La
Goutte d'or,* the opposition is that of the image and the sign. While these
two terms are often used as virtual synonyms in Western aesthetic
thinking, Tournier distinguishes between them. In *La Goutte d'or,* at
least, he construes the image as essentially figurative, as referring to
some model which actually exists in the physical world, and the sign as
an abstract form which has no explicit reference, but which evokes
everything. Zett Zobeida's golden droplet is a perfect example of this
sort of sign: 'la bulle dorée ne veut rien dire qu'elle-même. C'est le
signe pur, la forme absolue' (**31**); 'bijou abstrait, absolu, sans modèle
dans la nature' (**49**).

Basing himself on recent anthropological research, Tournier
associates the image with European culture and the sign with Islamic
culture, although he does recognise that this distinction does not hold
completely, as will be discussed more fully later. However, it is useful to
point out here that the golden droplet is itself appropriated by European
image-systems when it is compared to the Roman *bulla aurea* (**103**) and
is thereby endowed with explicit meaning.

Tournier's fascination with the image has two main sources. First,
his interest in photography—for years he produced a radio programme
on photography, he was a co-founder of the annual *Rencontres*

Photographiques in Arles, he knows most of the eminent contemporary photographers and has published books with several of them, and he is known as 'France's greatest amateur photographer' (the word 'amateur' both amuses and irritates him in this context). Second, his reading of the Bible. Throughout his works, we find rewritings of the Genesis story of the Creation, and he is especially fascinated—and worried—by the statement that God said 'Let us make man in our *image,* after our *likeness'* (*Genesis,* I: 26; my emphasis). The difference between 'image' and 'likeness' is the generating model for the philosophico-theological speculations in *Gaspard, Melchior et Balthazar,* and it informs many of the essays on contemporary art in *Le Tabor et le Sinaï* (1988). Tournier is haunted by the fact that Mosaic law, the ancient law of the Hebrews contained in the Pentateuch, prohibits images of God—who is unknown and unknowable, though omnipresent. However, he also knows that Saint Paul proclaims that Christ is the icon, that is to say both the image and the likeness, of God (see *2 Corinthians,* IV: 4). Christianity differs from other religions in its insistence on the Incarnation, on the fact that Christ is a physical *manifestation of God,* 'the Word [...] made flesh' (*John,* I: 14). In other words, Christ is an *authentic* image. Once God, in the person of Christ, has been seen, heard, touched, tasted, smelled, the ban on images can be lifted, and at the beginning of the seventh century, Pope Gregory declared that sacred images should be permitted because they are 'writings for the illiterate'.

While several contemporary thinkers such as Jean-François Lyotard may assert that we do not read images but experience them, Tournier adheres to the Gregorian position, believing that we read images, scanning them for their semantic content. (This position is justified by E.H. Gombrich's research into eye movement: he demonstrates that in the West, when we see an image, our eyes automatically—and for cultural reasons—scan from left to right, as we do when reading a page of writing). Yet there remains the problem of authenticity. How 'true' is the image? How 'true' can it be?

In Christian cultures, the classic case of the 'authentic' image is, of course, the Shroud of Turin, the veil with which St Veronica is said to have wiped Christ's face while he was on his way to Calvary and which bears an image of His features. Her very name is considered to be an anagrammatic formulation of 'true image' (*vera* + *icon*). This postulated anagram is problematic, in that it uses a Latin word and a Greek word. Furthermore, recent carbon-dating tests on the Shroud have cast doubts on its authenticity. Nonetheless, it remains one of the most revered relics in Christendom, and it generated one of Tournier's most important fictional texts on photography, 'Les Suaires de Véronique' in *Le Coq de bruyère* (1978), where he both overturns the traditional notion that Veronica represents the compassionate woman and aggressively contests the right of image-makers to be predatory.

The authenticity of an image depends on three criteria: firstly, the content of the image should give reliable information about the model; secondly, there should be a causal link between the model and the created image; thirdly, the code of the imagistic message should be familiar or accessible to the viewer. Barthes has suggested that the photographic image is a message without a code and is consequently a continuous message. He has also suggested that, when a text is added to an image, it must operate semantically from a position of parasitism. Tournier is primarily a writer, and so believes in the primacy of the text—or at least of reading. He also frequently, if playfully, articulates a belief in the transparency of the photographic image, stating that it reveals—neutrally and mechanistically—the relationship that links the subject to its image. In this, he is following a historical trend established by Zola amongst others—and it should be remembered, especially when reading *La Goutte d'or,* that Tournier consistently cites Zola as one of his main model, and that he has great admiration for Zola's photography, which he sees as significantly different from his writing. For instance,he writes in his essay 'Émile Zola photographe': 'Si Zola écrit avec son cerveau et son imagination, c'est avec son cœur qu'il photographie' (*CM,* 9). However, Tournier's own experience as a photographer and as a critic of photography has taught him that the great photographers are latter-day magicians, conjuring up the scenes they desire and imprinting a highly subjective mark on their images (see especially his comments in books created with Édouard Boubat and Arthur Tress).

These different attitudes are, of course, incompatible, as Tournier well knows, but one of the main strategies of *La Goutte d'or* is to play them against each other in order to offer a characteristic fusion of aesthetics and politics in a novelistic form.

Tournier has written that 'la ressemblance comprend tout l'être— corps et âme—tandis que l'image n'est qu'un masque superficiel et peut-être trompeur' (*GMB,* 47), and that 'L'image est toujours rétrospective. C'est un miroir tourné vers le passé' (*GMB,* 234). This elegiac view of the image is similar to those of Walter Benjamin, Roland Barthes and Susan Sontag, all of whom have proposed that the photograph is a *memento mori,* a (sentimental) souvenir of a reality which has disappeared for ever. Tournier himself also insists that 'la photographie veut *retenir,* c'est sa vocation, sa raison d'être' (*VP,* 208). These theorists share an awareness of the supposed non-intervention of the photographer in the images s/he creates, and all insist on the importance of chance (of the mechanical, the non-determined) in the creation of the image, yet they also recognise that the spectator will see things differently and will seek to find an authorial presence or trace.

Photographs may thus be read in the same way as one reads painted portraits or statues—as the site of a speculation, of a bet and of a questing (Pascalian) leap. So the much-vaunted transparency of the photographic image becomes a veil through which we see the existence that we know or want to see. Our initial, if deluded, belief in the photographer's impartiality and in the objective reality of the scene s/he presents is displaced by our own desires. We seek confirmation of our individual ideological positions, and therefore seek to find ourselves as much as the otherness of the image.

La Goutte d'or presents a series of commentaries on the function and meaning of photographs in the context of Western culture. Whether the photograph is taken by a tourist wanting a souvenir, by a commercial photographer pandering to the fantasies of his tourist clients, by a pimp photographing his blond prostitute in Saharan sand dunes in order to please both Frenchmen and Arab oil sheiks, or by an artist such as Étienne Milan, the subject is always a victim. When the novel's third blond Frenchwoman (the second prostitute Idriss encounters) asks her pimp if just for once she might see a photograph of the rich client who has selected her from her photographs, he aggressively reminds her that only he who pays has the right to choose from photos and that there is no possibility of reversing the roles. Her response is the angry—if vain—hope of all models, mainly women but also such innocent men as Idriss, who wish to redress the balance of photographic power:

> —Que vous le vouliez ou non, un jour je ferai mon choix. Et c'est pas sur photos que je le ferai. Ce sera en vrai, dans la vie.(**169**)

Like Idriss, the 'comic-strip' blond woman is ultimately powerless—'[une] esclave blonde' who has chosen 'la cage confortable' over 'la misère de la liberté' (**168**), a marionnette actuated by strings pulled by others. She can only dream of regaining the freedom she renounced when she allowed herself to be photographed, for the images of her have been irrevocably put into circulation and, even were she to meet 'un homme honnête [...] qui m'aime' (*ibid.*), she would always live in fear that these suggestive images 'lui sautent à la figure un jour ou l'autre' (*ibid.*)—although in a radically different way to that in which they 'sautent à la figure' of a client!

In a typical example of Tournierian over-determination, the blond prostitute is equated paradoxically both with Idriss's first photographer and with Idriss himself—and photographs are presented as more of a stigma than the tattoos which are an integral part of the Berber tradition. More importantly, this episode questions the difference between 'reality' and 'art', for it is difficult to determine exactly when the comic strip dialogue stops and the café conversation begins. Tournier worked lengthily on this scene, which he intended to be a

novelistic articulation of his belief that reality imitates art as much and
as often as art imitates reality. Idriss, the child of an anti-image culture,
is seduced by the apparent identity between representation and reality.
He therefore functions, albeit in a cautionary way, as a paradigm of
contemporary Western man who believes (in) the surface of visual
representations rather than seeking for their epistemological and/or
ontological meanings.

Another chance encounter leads the young Berber shepherd to the
two- room apartment of Étienne Milan who photographs shop-window
dummies, another form of 'esclaves' (**173**), in pastoral settings (with,
occasionally, live boys) in order to throw doubt on the reality of the
landscape. While Milan's workroom resembles a bizarre operating
theatre (echoes of Mary Shelley's *Frankenstein*!), his bedroom is more
like a charnel-house:

> La pièce évoquait une scène de massacre, ou encore le garde-manger de
> l'Ogre. [...] des piles de torses, des faisceaux de bras, des fagots de jambes
> soigneusement rangés contre les murs faisaient penser à un charnier d'un
> genre particulier, très propre, très sec, rendu plus ambigu encore par une
> ribambelle de têtes souriantes aux joues roses disposées sur des étagères.
> (**178**)

Idriss is amazed and somewhat frightened by what he sees. The reader
shares these reactions, yet those familiar with Tournier's works also
recognise the description as the site of a complex intertextual network.
The most obvious reference is to Gilles de Rais, the fifteenth-century
rapist and murderer of scores of young children and source for the
legend of Barbe-Bleue. In *Gilles & Jeanne,* Tournier presents Gilles as
the victim of an 'inversion maligne' after he has witnessed the burning
at the stake of Jeanne d'Arc, his former companion-at-arms. Tournier
in no way seeks to excuse Gilles's monstrous behaviour; indeed he
quotes extensively from the proceedings of Gilles's trial and himself
writes: 'Ce qui se perpétra alors jour après jour, nuit après nuit sous les
combles de Tiffauges dépasse en horreur ce que l'imagination la plus
dépravée peut concevoir' (*G&J*, 112). No detail is spared, yet the text
does more than reveal the scandalously erotic nature of Gilles's
paedophiliac sadism: it points up the tenderness which, paradoxically,
also informs his behaviour—as when he kisses the most beautiful of the
severed heads arranged on his mantelpiece (*ibid.,* 143). While refusing
to make moral judgements, Tournier suggests that Gilles suffered from
some grotesque displacement of paternal affection, just as, albeit in a
much less dangerous way, does Milan, who at one point sighs 'La
paternité...' (**179**).

The other main Tournierian Ogre is Abel Tiffauges in *Le Roi des
aulnes,* who defines himself on the first page of the novel as the mythic

Ogre, not merely as a metaphorical one, and who later comes to be
known as 'l'Ogre de Rominten' and 'l'Ogre de Kaltenborn'. He too loves
children, desiring above all to carry them and thereby to achieve a non-
erotic union with them—but he, by another 'inversion maligne', also
becomes responsible for finding and stealing children so that they can
become cannon-fodder for the Nazis.

A third Ogre is to be found in 'La Fugue du Petit Poucet', in *Le
Coq de bruyère*. His very name both evokes and palliates the baleful
resonances of Ogre: he is called Logre, but he is a pot-smoking gentle
giant whose most salient characteristic is his maternal gentleness. He is
therefore the 'inversion bénigne' of the Ogre—who does, however, give
marijuana joints to his seven daughters!

All three previous Ogres are therefore (at least) double, and our
reading of the description of Milan's bedroom and indeed of his sexual
fantasies cannot be adequate unless we recognise that reading should be
intertextual and that Tournier is playing with references to other of his
novels as well as with allusions to the Ogre of fairy tales. Furthermore,
Tournier is urging us to read in a non-judgemental way: for him, there
is no absolute morality, merely a series of culture-specific moralities.
Reading itself is, of course, a largely culture-specific process, but
Tournier believes that, when reading, we should attempt to liberate
ourselves from the chains of any single moral system. Only then can we
escape from the tyranny of the dominant political ideology. This is,
perhaps, the main message of *La Goutte d'or*.

There is one further intertextual reference which, though more
subtle, is crucial to an understanding both of this episode and of
Tournier's writing practice in general. It is to Géricault, who peopled
his studio with limbs and torsos procured from morgues as he prepared
his famous painting *Le Radeau de la Méduse* (1819). This work, one of
the greatest visual interpretations of human suffering, caused a political
scandal at the time, in that it was seen to be an attack on traditional
French values of fraternity and responsibility (and let us not forget that
Le Radeau de la Méduse is 'explained' to the wedding party in Zola's
L'Assommoir, which, with its setting in the rue de la Goutte d'Or—see
177) is an important intertext for *La Goutte d'or*!). What interests
Tournier is less the painting itself than the 'necrophiliac' nature of its
creation. Milan may be working with inanimate dummies, but his
fascination with dismembered bodies is a displacement of Géricault's
compulsive need to surround himself with (partial) corpses in order to
learn how to portray the living—and, in the process, to question the
very possibility of representing the body as an imitation, as a *mimesis*.

Milan's justification of his art is that it is a 'consécration' (**180**),
whereby the real is remembered and indeed revered through and in a
ritualistic act which proclaims its very artificiality. In this way,

something local and ephemeral becomes universal and eternal. In all his works, Tournier has speculated, almost obsessively, on the Mosaic interdict on image-making, yet he also clearly believes that images can be theologically and societally recuperated provided that they have the quality of a consecration. His primary model is the Eucharist, which does not reproduce but consecrates Christ's self-sacrifice, yet he frequently warns against the temptation of attempting to make literal the union with Christ that Christian theology advocates. For instance, in *Les Météores,* Alexandre discovers Thomas Koussek lying under a life-sized statue of Christ 'déshabillé de sa croix, mais non moins crucifié, car je distinguai bientôt Thomas couché sous lui, reproduisant son attitude, gémissant à demi écrasé par le poids de la statue' (*M,* 48). The text makes clear that Koussek, an expert in 'dry come' or orgasm with no release of sperm, desires an erotic union with Christ, but—significantly—it presents such a desire not only as a heretical act but, more importantly, as a misreading of the Biblical injunction. Another example is the young sculptor in *La Goutte d'or* who decides to use his own body as a model for the life-size crucifix he was commissioned to make: 'si j'avais une quelconque vocation mystique, je ne sais pas jusqu'où ce genre de plaisanterie pourrait me mener' (**184**).

In *Le Médianoche amoureux,* Tournier devotes several tales to a consideration of acts of commemoration in order ultimately to show how the marriage of Nadège and Yves can be saved—if only they can, like all couples, understand that the repetitious monotony of domestic life can also be viewed and lived as a series of commemorative consecrations of their wedding vows and of their initial commitment to each other. This may seem too 'clever', too convenient a way of justifying and rehabilitating repetition, but it both has deep cultural roots and also questions the nature of reality as we perceive it in our modern spectaclist society—where images have first become fetishised and then become commodities to be bought and sold.

Milan's decision to photograph dummies is grounded in such a socio-political belief. He explains to Idriss:

> Quant aux mannequins, étant eux-mêmes déjà des images, leur photo est une image d'image, ce qui a pour effet de doubler leur pouvoir dissolvant. Il en résulte une impression de rêve éveillé, d'hallucination vraie. C'est absolument la réalité sapée à sa base par l'image. (**181**)

While persuasive in its own right, this argument involves us once more in an intertextual exploration. The use of 'rêve' reminds of many of Milan's photographer predecessors in the novel—with the difference that he adds the epithet 'éveillé'. In other words, like the Surrealist poets and painters, Milan seeks to establish a state of lucidity-within-dream or of *in-between-ness*—and to challenge the authority of the image. His

equation of dummies with twins (**177-8**) is undoubtedly a willed
misreading by Tournier of the myth of the Androgynes which, first
advanced in Plato's *Symposium,* explains why we are constantly looking
for our 'other half'. It also evokes the lengthy analysis of twin-ness in
Les Météores, which, though substantially based on the work of the
psychologist René Zazzo, goes beyond the psychological to erect a
theory of 'the copy of the copy', wherein the last copy is posited as
always superior to its predecessor and even to the original. In this
respect, Tournier's posoition is close to that of Borges (whom he has
never read!), since both proclaim the aesthetic value of irony in any
copy. However, in *La Goutte d'or,* the 'copy of the copy' theory is re-
evaluated in political terms. When Idriss accepts to be the model for
Maghrebi-type shop-window dummies, his image is stolen once again—
and this time in 3-D. He therefore, naïvely, passively, renounces the
right to be someone who sees and becomes someone who will be seen:
an image without individuality. Once the cast has been made, he no
longer counts. Like any *Vogue* model, like any pop star, like the
Princess of Wales..., he will henceforward be judged by his consonance
with the images that have been made of him. He has become a
commodity which can and will be mechanistically reproduced as long as
he corresponds to the desires and fantasies of the buying public. And,
having lost his eyelashes and eyebrows in the bowl of alginate (**186**), his
only future is to imitate the jerky movements of an automated dummy:
the commercial viability of the mechanical has taken from the creative
gratuitousness of the individual.

Throughout Tournier's work, we find characters whose narcissistic
drives lead them to speculate on what they see and, especially, to attempt
to identify completely with the object of their gaze—even if they have
to manipulate this image by giving only a partial reading of it. The
consequence of this is that the artistic image *qua* image or icon is
rejected. The spectator becomes more important than the image. In *Les
Météores* (pp. 372-6),Tournier suggested that an obsessional desire to
identify completely with an image must lead to death. The argument in
La Goutte d'or is more complex. Idriss is usually chosen by other
people as their model; in other words, he is their victim, their prey. He
does not see first, but is seen—seen by the gaze and by the desire of the
other. Even when he has his photograph taken in an automatic booth, he
is betrayed by the machine which, though theoretically impartial and
mechanical, gives him pictures of a bearded man (**94-5**). Although he
attempts to convince himself that he might have had a beard before
leaving Tabelbala, later on the car ferry he replies to the goldsmith who
warns him that he had better grow a beard in order to avoid having
problems with customs and police officials: 'Ce serait pire, je n'en ai
presque pas. Et puis tout de même, ce n'est pas à moi de ressembler ma

photo. C'est ma photo qui doit me ressembler, non?' (**100**). This reveals that Idriss is a reader, albeit a naïve one, who believes that the photographic image is a neutral reproduction of reality. Tournier certainly does not share this belief. Already in *Le Roi des aulnes*, he defines the painter as 'expansif, généreux, centrifuge' and the photographer as 'avare, avide, gourmand, centripète' (*RA*, 168). And he accords to his photographing central character, Abel Tiffauges, a sexual and predatory attitude which he elaborates in many of his later works:

> Je me plais ainsi équipé d'un sexe énorme, gainé de cuir, dont l'œil de Cyclope s'ouvre comme l'éclair quand je lui dis «Regarde!» et se referme inexorablement sur ce qu'il a vu. Merveilleux organe, voyeur et mémorant, faucon diligent qui se jette sur sa proie lui voler et rapporter au maître ce qu'il y a en elle de plus profond et de plus trompeur, son apparence! (*R A*, 167)

The photographer is therefore perceived as a thief within the context of Western aesthetics—and I would note in passing that theft ('le vol') occurs in almost all of Tournier's texts, usually in the context of an aesthetic or a sexual encounter, both of which invariably involve a hierarchical relationship of superior to inferior or predator to prey. In this context, it is important to remember that the blond tourist 'portait une chemisette kaki très échancrée et un short outrageusement court' and that she 'brandissait un appareil de photo' (**13**). She is therefore presented as a phallic woman: sexualised, yet castrating.

This inscription of a form of violence into artistic and erotic relations, which is characteristic of Tournier's work, may have its origins in his traumatic childhood experience of tonsillotomy,[1] but it is also determined by his reading of Gide's work (notably of *L'Immoraliste,* Gide's various journals and the correspondence). The influence of Gide is found most explicitly in his story 'Aventures africaines' in *Le Médianoche amoureux* (pp. 139-44), but in many of his other writings Tournier exploits the Gidean (anti-) ethic which justifies mercenary attitudes and theft within an erotic relationship. However, if the Gidean position is essentially one of voyeurism, Tournier prefers to insist on the fact that when a richer and older man condones theft or exploitation, this subverts the simplicity of the master / servant relationship.

In *La Goutte d'or,* Idriss is occasionally given money, yet he never achieves the independence and authority of Abdallah in 'Aventures africaines' (the question of his sexual initiation will be considered in the next chapter). Paradoxically, whether others steal from him (notably the blond woman photographer who steals his image and the blond Marseille prostitute who steals his golden droplet) or give to him, he

[1] See *Le Vent Paraclet,* pp 17-19; and Michael Worton, 'Use and Abuse of Metaphor in Tournier's *Le Vol du vampire', Paragraph,* 10 (1987), pp. 13-28.

always remains a victim—and, more importantly, incomplete. His mother says to him when learning that he has been photographed, 'C'est un peu de toi qui est parti' (**22**). Idriss has manipulated the truth of his encounter and told his mother, who is 'toujours portée à imaginer le pire', that there were two men in the Land Rover (*ibid.*). His mother and her neighbour Kuka ben Laïd are certain that his photograph will never be sent to him and so prophesy with resignation that he will leave in quest of it. His uncle Mogadem, a former army corporal, later tells him of how his own photograph 'saved' his life and affirms 'Non tu vois, les photos, faut les garder. Faut pas les laisser courir!' (**56**). While these two positions may seem initially identical, they are radically different. The women who have never left the oasis believe wholly in the interdiction of images: for them, a camera is a form of the Evil Eye, so Idriss is cursed, destined to leave Tabelbala. Uncle Mogadem, who has fought in Italy, explicitly articulates his contempt for the superstitious attitude of the older members of the oasis community, yet he is in his own (oppositional) way just as superstitious, hence his encouragement to Idriss to depart and find his image. There is, however, a blank, an Idriss-willed silence in both these attitudes: the fact that his photographer was both a woman and a blond European. So (sexual) desire may be waiting, like a time-bomb, to explode the concept of binary oppositions.

In several earlier works, Tournier has sought to establish a difference between *destin* (a fate decided by outside forces) and *destinée* (a self-created fate). The first great avatar in French literature of this duality is perhaps Racine's *Phèdre,* in which Phèdre is cursed by Vénus but finally judges herself and chooses her own death. Another, more recent example is Zola's novel cycle *Les Rougon-Macquart,* where the apparently inexorable laws of heredity are opposed to the attempts of protagonists to establish an autonomous life. All of Tournier's novels are, in some ways, structured by the *destin/destinée* opposition, but Idriss is different from his Tournierian predecessors in that he has neither the wish nor the ability to read what he sees. Rather, he desires to find—and identify with—the one image of himself that he will never see: the photograph taken (stolen) by the blond tourist. For him, there can be no alternative to *destin* until he has been persuaded by others and especially by his experiences that *destinée* demands a personal and *active* commitment.

Until the last pages of the novel he is passive, a marionnette manipulated by a variety of other people who project onto him their own fantasies and needs. He is, as Tournier has often said, a modern Candide, an innocent who has not (yet) learned to read the text that is the world. His essential question is 'qui suis-je?' This question is the 'non-dit' that underpins the entire novel. Repeatedly posed in both personal and cultural terms, it is perhaps best understood by reference to Breton's *Nadja*, where the initial 'qui suis-je?' means both 'Who am I?' and 'Who am I following?' Idriss is searching not only for himself, but for an absence—and, though he does not know it, for a means of making that absence fully, irrevocably absent. With no inculcated intellectual apparatus to aid him, he is striving to achieve a form of absence which re-inscribes presence—and indeed, guarantees it.

He may seek to see and to decode the signs around him, but his search is pre-determined to fail. First, because the Islamic sign is abstract and therefore defies decoding. Second, because the European sign which haunts all of Tournier's work is posited as semantically potent and is usually perceived as a prophecy or a portent. In *Le Roi des aulnes*, Tiffauges writes that 'Tout est signe' (*RA*, 15), and Tournier chooses as the epigraph to the third chapter, 'Hyperborée', a statement by Claudel:

> Tout ce qui passe est promu à la dignité d'expression, tout ce qui se passe est promu à la dignité de signification. Tout est symbole ou parabole. (*RA*, 248)

In other words, the European sign is meaningful in a radically different way from the Islamic sign: it is meant to be ultimately understood within a precise situation, whereas the abstract Islamic sign evokes, but does not explain, the meaningfulness of the world. How, then, can a young Berber be expected to read signs in a European way?

Idriss may have been educated to believe that images are necessarily harmful (**24-5**), but he has no training in seeing. Just as Tiffauges has his mentor in the shape of an older boy (Nestor), Idriss, the sedentary oasis-dweller, has Ibrahim, the archetypal nomad. It is, though, by no means innocent that Ibrahim has only one eye. His unerring aim when throwing stones at crows or fennecs testifies to a predatory accuracy and his perception of Idriss is that of a cynical master:

> son œil pétillait de lueurs ironiques, parce qu'Idriss n'était qu'un niais d'oasien, une 'queue ronde', docile, doux, mais de peu de poids en face d'un chamelier chaamba (**16**)

This apparently episodic passage has a programmatic function. We certainly find the characteristic Tournierian privileging of the nomad over the sedentary. We also find sexuality used as a means of establishing difference—and indeed, superiority. Most pertinently, Ibrahim is capable of seeing ironically. This means that, while he is in many ways Idriss's alter ego, he can actually see beyond himself and see (and judge) another person as other—and as whole. Most of the people Idriss encounters on his quest for his personal Grail are physically or emotionally blind, unable to see beyond their own fragmented fantasies. Lala Ramirez, who takes Idriss for her dead son Ismaïl, has eyes without eyelashes, eyes which never close, 'un regard immobile' (**91**), a 'regard de reptile' (**92**), a 'regard de presbyte' (**93**)—images which both indicate her 'blind' monomania and evoke the mechanical, unjudging lens of a camera. Lala had left her origins in 'un sud indéterminé' to marry 'chrétiennement' a building contractor from Oran who was 'd'origine espagnole' (**90**). Like Idriss, she has therefore partially abandoned her roots and spends her life moving literally and figuratively between Arab culture and Christian culture, between Béchar and Oran. The tragedies in her life have driven her to madness. However, as the reader realizes after reading the first chapters, *La Goutte d'or* is largely structured by a series of prophetic events, whose significance is, alas, not perceived by Idriss until he finally engages in a celebratory dance of reintegration with his pneumatic drill/Zett Zobeida. The Lala episode is a warning, which is explicitly reiterated by the young goldsmith on the car ferry, who tells Idriss that it is dangerous to reject one's religion:

> Là où nous allons, la religion est plus nécessaire que chez nous.Tu vas te trouver entouré d'étrangers, d'indifférents, d'ennemis. Contre le désespoir et la misère, tu n'auras peut-être que le Coran et la mosquée. (**99**)

The novel is saturated by references to eyes and seeing. Several of these are apparently episodic, as in the case of Mustapha, the 'artiste photographe' who is 'très myope' (**82**) and the blond prostitute/model he meets in a Paris café who is also 'myope' (**169**); of the lorry driver on the car-ferry whose 'yeux de porcelaine bleue' are as unseeing as those of a doll (**100**); of the Marseille prostitute who draws a black eyeliner under her 'faux cils' so that her eyes will be *seen* rather than function as organs of sight; or of the young man Philippe who sits opposite Idriss in the Paris train: 'Il le regardait, toujours souriant, sans le voir. Idriss le dévorait des yeux' (**113**). Idriss is throughout striving to see, but he has no model to guide him, not since Ibrahim died in the well.

In Paris he meets Monsieur Mage who sees—but not straight!: 'Son regard, cassé par un léger strabisme, l'observe à travers des lunettes à grosse monture' (**138**). When Mage later stares at Idriss, this 'aggrave son strabisme' (**141**). Although he denies that he actually has a squint, preferring the term 'une coquetterie dans le regard', Mage has been nicknamed 'Biglou' by the young Arabs who mercilessly exploit his homosexuality (**144**). A director of advertising commercials, Mage is in the business of creating seductive images for others, but, like Idriss, he has not yet learned to reconcile himself to the image others have of him: 'Je vois dans les yeux des garçons l'image d'une grosse tante sentimentale, bigleuse et bourrée d'argent. Je n'arrive pas à me persuader que c'est moi' (145). He may see well enough to warn Idriss against being sucked into Zob's 'cheptel' (livestock!) of prostitutes (140), but the force of his own sexual needs and fantasies prevent him from becoming the mentor or model that Idriss needs.

All of Tournier's novels are so carefully crafted that some critics have accused him of over-determining his readers' responses and thereby denying the creativity of reading. This accusation has been directed especially at *La Goutte d'or* because of its 'obvious' proleptic structure and narrative circularity. Such readings, however, are blind to the emotional force of the novel which encourages its readers both to judge Idriss and to identify with him—to identify themselves as 'bad' or, at best, naïve, readers.

The narration suggests that Idriss's quest for himself can begin really to advance only when he admits that sight is less important than insight. The mentor Idriss needs is, paradoxically, someone he never meets: the old, blind—and unnamed—Arab whom Amouzine helps to the front row of a concert by Oum Kalsoum. Significantly, he wears the traditional turban and djellaba and his blindness 'inspire une crainte respectueuse' in a predominantly African audience (195). He cannot physically see the singer (whose own life was radically transformed when her photograph was first published in a newspaper), but he can imagine and construct her mentally. When Amouzine asks him how he 'sees' her, his response is revelatory:

> «Verte!» m'a-t-il dit. Cet aveugle de naissance voyait notre chanteuse nationale comme une couleur, la couleur verte! Et il a précisé: «Sa voix a autant de nuances que tout le vert de la nature, et le vert est la couleur du Prophète!» (196)

An exile in France, the blind Arab proclaims his ethnic origins through the garb he chooses to wear and, more importantly, he understands that Oum Kalsoum, a fat lady with her heavy face hidden under thick dark glasses, is a symbol, a sign of and for Islam. And this is because he does not see her as an individual but hears in her songs the primal murmurs of his personal and cultural past. She can therefore be for him an embodiment of what Lessing calls in *Laocoon* the *pregnant moment* (German: *fruchtbar*), an artistic instant when all absences become present and when the totally abstract and the totally concrete fuse.

Idriss's mistake is to search only for the the concrete, *lisible* meaning of images, whereas Islamic signs, such as Zett's golden droplet, have an essentially abstract quality: consequently they are *scriptible* and will always defy any reductive reading or writing.[2] Idriss is a paradigm of what we all live in our modern multi-cultural societies: he slowly comes

---

[2] For a definition of these terms, see Roland Barthes, *S/Z* (Seuil, 1970), p. 10.

to realize that no image is 'true' and that the portrait is the least reliable of all images, since it promises the opposite of what it can offer. One reason for this is that we can rarely have a full understanding (or, indeed, acceptance) of the code that infuses the image-message. Another is that, in the novel, every image is determined or mediated by 'la race des blondes voleuses de photo et de goutte d'or' (**116**).

How then can Western Europeans read the novel? Inevitably we must read it from a (post-) Judeo-Christian position, yet the narration insistently challenges the appropriateness of our doing so. Furthermore, it asks whether we can even think we have the right to judge Idriss. The novel poses these questions and deliberately offers no clear-cut answers, preferring to interrogate the nature of Western reading. Above all, it demands a political reading.

As I have suggested, Tournier both is and is perceived as a political maverick. It may therefore be appropriate to read his novel through the prism of political theory—although my reading in no way intends to suggest that the author hidden behind his text is Marxist, socialist or whatever!

In *La Société du spectacle,* an assault on the ways in which Western society has been enslaved by images, the Situationist Guy Debord states that 'le spectacle est la principale production de la société actuelle'.[3] By 'spectacle', he means not 'un ensemble d'images, mais un rapport social entre des personnes, médiatisé par des images' (Debord, 10); spectacle is and involves 'l'effacement des limites du moi et du monde par l'écrasement du moi qu'assiège la présence-absence du monde', it is 'l'effacement du vrai et du faux' (Debord, 169). Debord's radical attitude towards society may be politically disquieting, but he is surely right in his assertion that in 'the West' image-making has taken over from serious dialogue or the sharing of discourses. Politicians have recognised this. So, in order to win an election, George Bush will don an assortment of silly but 'vote-winning' hats, François Mitterrand will pose with writers and their books, Margaret Thatcher will remove the (carefully-scattered) litter in St James's Park with a gardener's spike— all for the benefit of the cameras of the press. The 'photo-opportunity' has become a tyrannical imposition which enables marketing specialists to sell their goods (we only ever see the pre-programmed image, whatever the reality of the photo-session may have been). In Britain in 1991 and 1992, all the party political broadcasts chose to market brands rather than to conduct argument. The party supremos had learned, especially after the last U.S. Presidential election, that only images count—especially if they are accompanied by a 'sound-bite' that can hit the front pages of the newspapers and the television news programmes.

---

[3] Guy Debord, *La Société du spectacle* (Éditions Gérard Lebovici, 1987 [1967]), p. 14. All further page references to this will follow in the text, preceded by 'Debord'.

Following the American example, the British political parties hired film
directors who were experts in Hollywoodese—and the French political
parties have followed suit.

While *La Goutte d'or* is Tournier's most extended diatribe against
modern Western spectaclist society, he has for many years been warning
of its dangers in his literary texts as well as in his interviews. Two
passages will serve as exempla. The first is from his essay 'Touche' in
Des clefs et des serrures (1979):

> Ne touche pas! L'odieuse injonction qui retentit cent fois par jour aux
> oreilles de l'enfant fait de lui un *aveugle*, un chien sans flair, errant
> tristement dans un monde où tout est enfermé dans des vitrines. [...] Notre
> société hygiénique et puritaine se montre de moins en moins favorable à la
> connaissance et aux satisfactions tactiles. Toucher avec ses yeux. [...] Les
> lieux de contact érotiques sont interdits ou infestés de surveillance. En
> même temps se développe une inflation galopante d'images. Le magazine, le
> film, la télévision gavent l'œil et réduisent le reste de l'homme au néant.
> L'homme d'aujourd'hui se promène muselé et manchot dans un *palais de
> mirages.*
>
> Parfois, tout de même, un pavé vole dans une vitrine et un jeune corps
> se rue sur les fruits défendus... (*CS*, 25-6; my emphasis)

The second is from one of his recent theoretical essays on writing and
reading in *Le Vol du vampire:*

> Nous subissons tous la pression du corps social qui nous impose comme
> autant de stéréotypes nos conduites, nos opinions et jusqu'à notre aspect
> extérieur. Le propre des créateurs est de résister à cette sujétion pour
> remonter le courant et mettre en circulation leurs propres modèles. (*VV*, 25)

Idriss is always separated from the reality he desires to establish or
re-find by a 'vitrine', be this a shop-window, the lens of a camera, a
peep-show one-way mirror or the fantasising gaze of another person.
Soon after Idriss arrives in Paris, the narrator makes one of his many
interpretative interventions, explaining to the reader, in a paragraph
saturated with references to *vitrines,* the implications for an immigrant
of the society of spectacle:

> Il y avait eu des *vitrines* du musée saharien de Béni Abbès. Mais en vérité
> depuis son arrivée à Paris, Idriss ne faisait qu'aller *de vitrine en vitrine.*
> [...] La *vitrine* signale un commerce d'un niveau relevé. Encore faut-il
> qu'elle ne se ramène pas à une simple fenêtre par laquelle on plonge dans
> l'intérieur du magasin avec son patron, sa caisse et le manège des clients.
> Non, une vitrine digne de ce nom est fermée par une cloison. Elle forme un
> lieu clos, à la fois totalement étalé aux regards, mais inaccessible aux mains,
> impénétrable et sans secret, un monde où l'on ne touche qu'avec les yeux,
> et cependant réel, nullement illusoire comme celui de la photographie ou de
> la télévision. Coffre-fort fragile et provocant, *la vitrine appelle l'effraction.*
> (**160**; my emphasis)

The reference to 'effraction' or breaking and entering is, of course, prophetic, prefiguring the splitting of the window of CRISTOBAL and Co in the place Vendôme (**220**). More importantly, the paragraph is a call to readers to engage simultaneously in a process of identification with Idriss and in a process of identification with the narrator as an analytic commentator.

This double appeal serves to make us recognise that Idriss is a paradigm of all of us who live in the modern Western world. His first real glimpse of French society occurs on the ferry-boat when he sees on television 'la première image venant directement de France' (**103**). And what do he and his fellow immigrants see? Advertisements for life insurance, for *Soleil* washing powder, and for *Briodent* toothpaste. The immigrants do not understand the puns and image-associations so indispensable to European advertising campaigns (here, *Briodent* subliminally evokes 'Brille aux dents' and suggests that use of the produce will give *brio* to its users), but merely see the pictures. Each advert presents images of happy, smiling people, thereby reinforcing the ideology that European imperialistic powers have imposed on their former colonies, an ideology that the immigrants continue deludedly to believe. They may ask 'C'est donc cela la France?', but as soon as another televisual image appears, 'tout le monde se tait' (**104**). In other words, the image does not merely replace speech: it annuls it—hence the decision of political parties throughout the Western world to use advertising campaigns rather than public debate to attempt to ensure their election.

One of the main problems Idriss encounters from his initial meeting with the blond photographer is that he is essentially confronted with two categories of image: French-made images of France and French-made images of Arab culture. Even his pilgrimage in search of his photograph is charted in advance by the Frenchwoman (**14**). While it is important for the reader to remember that Idriss is a Berber and so only marginally or tangentially an Arab, he is perceived in France solely as an Arab immigrant. Tournier's text repeatedly reminds us of the specific origins of his protagonist, but the Europeans whom Idriss meets see him almost exclusively as an Arab boy who must conform to their ideological image.

This means that the images of 'himself' that he encounters are no more or other than semiotic signs of Arab culture produced within—and by—dominant French culture. Many Marxist theories insist that individual existence is determined by the intersection of differing social interests and by the refractions of reality that these entail. Tournier is in no way Marxist, but he does admit the worth of theories which posit class struggle as a determining factor in the formation of the individual subject. Here, again, he is influenced by the thinking, writing and political interventions of the spokesman for literary Naturalism. His.reading of Zola may be partial and projective, but it is clear from his many comments on him that he regards Zola's novelistic and theoretical presentations of the determinism of heredity and environment as forerunners of more recent social theories of oppression. However, in *La Goutte d'or*, he makes clear that he believes that cultural difference and the impulse to establish identity (ant-) agonistically are just as crucial to the process of subject formation. Idriss is systematically faced with image-makers, all of whom he accepts as authorities. He thus becomes the prey of the image-making machine that is Western society—but each time that he is confronted by another desiring spectator, a differently coloured filter-fragment of French ideology covers the lens of the eye or the camera that scans him. None of his predators wants him for the same reason, yet all share a desire to capture for themselves what they see as his otherness. This otherness is his ethnic difference, but, crucially, no one actually sees him as an individual: he is merely an image of the North African. In other words, Idriss, who has come to France in search of his identity, is repeatedly denied an autonomous existence and is perceived only as a stereotype. While he may refuse to accept as authentic reflections of him any of the images projected onto him, he is powerless to rebel and to affirm his specificity, firstly because he has not yet found or established it, and secondly because French culture promulgates refracted images of 'the Arab'—who is societally coded as inferior:

> —Les Français, commentait Achour, faut pas croire qu'ils nous aiment pas. Ils nous aiment à leur façon. Mais à condition qu'on reste à terre. Faut qu'on soit humble, minable. Un Arabe riche et puissant, les Français supportent pas ça. [...] Non, un Arabe, ça doit rester pauvre. Les Français sont charitables avec les pauvres Arabes, surtout les Français de gauche. Et ça leur fait tellement plaisir de se sentir charitables! (**123**)

The novel paints an accurate picture of what North African immigrants may experience in France, although Tournier permits himself some jokes—as when he situates Mage's location shoot in the rue Richomme (i.e. *riche homme*)! Much more than a documentary intervention into political debates, however, the text challenges each and every discourse of power by presenting Idriss as a figure of the naïve or passive reader. He does not understand what he sees or is given. This is because he is excluded from dominant French culture, whose discourses are alien to him. In their analyses of modern European political structures, Marxist theorists such as Gramsci insist on the concept—and the reality—of hegemony. As a post-imperialist society, as a permanent member of the United Nations Security Council and as a highly vocal policy-making member of the E.C., France is one of the most powerful hegemonic European cultures, this being reinforced by the fact that a third of the members of the United Nations communicate in French. However, we should remember that hegemony is rarely sustained by a single, unified ruling class; rather, its societal force is underpinned and created by a conjunction of complicit class fractions. One appropriate example of this is the recent convergence of French political statements on immigration, whereby virtually all parties have espoused an anti-immigration stance—in order to gain votes and consequently to maintain their control over ideology. The discourses of dominant ideology collude in the process of determining which images should be either included or excluded. The result of this is that, even though they do have somewhat different perspectives and projects, they not only prevent other discourses from acquiring any publicly recognised force but also keep such 'minorities' as immigrants in a state of subservience, silence and even invisibility.

Idriss in Paris is 'le Candide qui débarque', as Tournier has said in radio interviews. He is naïve, even innocent, and discovers that Paris does not correspond to the image he had of it in Tabelbala. Rather, he finds himself in a hall of mirrors (see **159**) wherein every image of himself is refracted through the prism of dominant French culture—and therefore unrecognisable. Tournier's fascination with mirrors informs thematically many of his other works, notably *Les Météores, Le Médianoche amoureux* and *Miroirs* (1973), an album with photographs by Édouard Boubat, and while all his novels have a circular structure, they also use mirroring as a structural device whereby episodes prefigure or reflect other episodes. Idriss's initiatory passage through the kaleidoscope of French images of North Africa evokes intertextually a crucial scene in *Journal du voleur* (1949) by Jean Genet, another writer much concerned with questións of colour, marginality and politics (notably *Les Nègres* [1958] and *Un captif amoureux* [1986]). In *Journal du voleur,* Genet's (anti-) hero Stilitano is presented as physically trapped in a hall of mirrors, whereas Idriss's kaleidoscopic cage is metaphorical, but both characters experience the same sensation of separation from the self. And through an inevitable, if partial identification with them, the reader learns to rethink Stendhal's celebrated assertion in *Le Rouge et le Noir* that 'un roman est un miroir qui se promène sur une grande route' (Book II, Ch. 19): all mirrors distort—especially when their specularity is 'truquée d'avance' by the ideological glaziers who are our political masters.

Idriss has neither the knowledge, the power nor the desire to create his own 'honest' mirror. He is condemned by the society he has 'chosen' to be just one more shard of glass in the kaleidoscope, to conform to its expectations and, ultimately, to be seen as nothing more than a 'divertissement'. And he will never even be able to turn the kaleidoscope's tube himself, since he is systematically objectified and deprived of the right to see and to speak. He always remains the object of the gaze of dominant French culture—until he accidentally causes the splitting of the CRISTOBAL and Co shop-window. Like many immigrants from France's former colonies, Idriss passively accepts the definition of the coloniser. As an individual, he may question the validity of French views of North Africans, yet his own sign-based culture has not prepared him for a battle with the image-based culture of Europe. He therefore capitulates to the barrage of images and to their founding ideology.

In *Portrait du colonisé*, the black activist Albert Memmi argues that the colonised 'commence par s'accepter [...] comme négativité' and 'n'arrive presque jamais à coïncider avec lui-même'.[4] This insight helps us to understand why Idriss must, in *La Goutte d'or*, remain passive. He can neither choose to subscribe to the discourses of dominant French ideology nor engage in a challenge to its hegemonic power; he is unable to accept the societally preferred French readings of the North African just as he is incapable of decoding them in a counter-hegemonic way, and consequently is resistant to final assimilation into the image-making machine. All he is permitted to do as a reader devoid of critical acumen and historical and intercultural knowledge is to negotiate his way blindly through the hall of mirrors which is created by politicians and supported by the media. He does not realise (though the reader does—or should!) that all the images he sees are reproduced by dominant French ideology which seeks to haul him into place not as a free subject but as an object. His essential problem is that he is between ideologies, and not until he has consciously re-embraced his oasis Berber culture can he establish an identity in France which will enable him to defend himself against the prevailing anti-Arab practices of ideological subjection.

---

[4] Albert Memmi, *Portrait du colonisé* (Éditions Jean-Jacques Pauvert, 1966), pp. 173, 175.

Chapter Three

Rites of passage:
initiation, sexuality and reading

All of Tournier's novels are quest-stories and initiation narratives. His protagonists are invariably presented as struggling to define themselves against political or cultural systems which threaten to enslave them, although in each case the menacing ideology is different. In *Vendredi*, Robinson works to establish an alternative to eighteenth-century European capitalism; in *Le Roi des aulnes,* Tiffauges eventually learns that his obsession with 'la phorie' or (child-) carrying can be realised—and non-sexually—without any collusion with Nazi anti-Semitism or 'master-race' ideology; in *Les Météores,* Alexandre, Jean, and Paul come to understand in different ways that their societal marginality is not necessarily an obstacle to the creation of a self-willed identity; in *Gaspard, Melchior et Balthazar,* the four Magi are led, after their encounter with the Christ-Child (or in Taor's case, with stories of the Messiah and ultimately with the table abandoned after the Last Supper), to repudiate both Roman and Hebrew politico-religious ideologies; in *Gilles & Jeanne,* Gilles de Rais accepts his execution at the stake only once he has internalised the phantasy of a mystical union with Jeanne d'Arc and, through her, with Christ—or at least with the Christian Divine; in *La Goutte d'or,* Idriss finds himself by forgetting France and 'losing himself' in his dance with the pneumatic drill—which permits him both to forget temporarily the image-making discourses of dominant French culture and to remember his cultural origins.

Each of these novels ends in a moment of sublimation and transmogrification—as do most of Tournier's short stories. This may be seen as sentimentality on the part of the novelist, but it is certain that one cannot understand Tournier's project unless one recognises that he believes in the possibility of self-transformation. Trained as a philosopher, Tournier understands that all dialectics have a creative potential, hence the mirror structure of his novels. More importantly, his reading of Hegel and of post-Hegelian thinkers taught him that dialectical argument is sterile unless there is at least the possibility of an *Aufhebung,* of a transcendence of binary oppositions. Idriss's quest ends, as does that of so many of Tournier's protagonists, in a transcendence of the systems that had threatened to imprison him.

However, he himself is not fully aware of the full import of what he is experiencing: he certainly rejects all that has been thrust at him, but he does this in a passive way, enclosing himself in a hermetic bubble of memories.

The novel maps a voyage of discovery and so has been described as a *Bildungsroman*. The appropriateness of this appellation will be considered in detail later; at this point, it is essential to consider how the novel's last paragraph functions. While Idriss may continue to be naïve, readers are denied this possibility, for the text problematises his rejection of European culture by explicitly activating intratextual resonances and thereby reminding us that we should be better readers of the novel than Idriss is of his own adventures. Indeed, I would argue that *La Goutte d'or* is as much about how one does, can (and should!) read as about how one responds to political or ideological systems.

At the end of the novel, Idriss is employed in the construction of an underground car park in the ultra-chic Place Vendôme which will 'engloutir jusqu'à 900 voitures' (217; my emphasis). This metaphor evokes the engulfment of the she-camel and of Ibrahim in the well at the beginning of the tale (20-21), thereby alerting the reader to the novel's narrative circularity. By functioning simultaneously and self-consciously as the closure and as a re-opening of the text, the final paragraph reminds us forcefully that Idriss's nascent discovery of himself is the result of what Tournier calls in *Le Roi des aulnes* 'un progrès à rebours', a looking backward in order ultimately to move forward creatively:

> Idriss danse toujours avec en tête une fantasmagorie de libellules, de criquets et de bijoux agités d'une trépidation forcenée. [...] Sourd et aveugle, Idriss continue à danser devant la goutte d'or avec sa cavalière pneumatique. (220).

The narrative ends thus with Idriss's forgetting of his surroundings and of his socio-economic reality as his past phantastically informs or inhabits his present. The ambiguities of his responses at the Berber wedding celebrations (28-31) are not wholly negated, but the reader is driven to re-read these pages in an attempt to understand why and how Idriss can escape from the tyranny of dominant French ideology, especially since it was at the wedding that Idriss began to '[se sentir] des ailes lui pousser aux talons' and consciously to repudiate the 'enracinement' of oasis culture.

The epithets 'sourd' and 'aveugle' are crucial, for Idriss has always been passive: deaf to what others have said to him and blind to the visual information with which he was presented. While all of Tournier's novels are narratively over-determined and saturated by intratextual and intertextual references, *La Goutte d'or* proclaims its internal structuring

more explicitly than any of its predecessors—in order to activate a
reading that will question the authority of the narration itself and, in
turn, of all political discourses. On the last page, Idriss's deafness and
blindness narratively represent a sense of alienation—from everything
around him, especially from exploitative and spectaclist French society.

Narratologically, however, they function differently, since both these
states of sensory deprivation have earlier been textually coded as
creative states of Arabic solidarity. The crowds welcoming Oum
Kalsoum throughout the Arab world shout: «Depuis que je te connais, je
suis sourd, je n'entends que ta voix, je suis muet, je ne parle que de toi!»
(193), Amouzine's 'protégé' at her Paris concert is feared and respected
by the crowd precisely because he is blind, and he is chosen by Oum
Kalsoum as the individual for whom she will sing (196). The text
equates Idriss with the blind man, albeit negatively, in that neither have
actually physically seen Oum Kalsoum, and so suggests that blindness
and indeed deafness are not necessarily passive states of inadequacy, but
may serve as aggressive defences against the Western obsession with
imagistic reproductions.

Idriss's voyage of discovery has not ended, though, at the end of the
novel, for he has merely undergone a series of experiences without
choosing—or assuming responsibility for—his acts. The final
hallucinatory dance with the pneumatic drill/Zett Zobeida is therefore a
narrative ending, since Idriss is oblivious to all around him: he and the
reader have merely encountered a chain of events. In order to establish
and assume their own individual identity (Idriss as a Berber, the reader
as a co-creator of the text), they should both start again from the
beginning and retrace Idriss's steps. They must learn to read properly,
that is to say in a hermeneutic or interpretative way, perceiving the
patterns and networks of images that give coherence to Idriss's
apparently disparate adventures.

The opening sentences of the novel have a programmatic function.
Idriss herds a flock of sheep and goats, days for him can pass 'comme
un rêve' he is fifteen years old and suffers from 'l'angoisse de la
solitude', he has memories of the legends handed down orally from the
days when the nomads made forays on the peasant populations of the
oases, he is hungry for 'un contact humain', and he is friendly with a
young Chaamba camel-herd, Ibrahim (9-10). These details seem
initially to be no more than exposition or scene-setting, yet, as the novel
progresses, we come to realise that they are keys to Idriss's identity,
which also prefigure his destiny. Like all of Tournier's protagonists,
Idriss is 'un marginal': he may enjoy spending time with Baba and
Mabrouk but they are no more than 'compagnons' whereas Ibrahim,
from the semi-nomadic Chaamba tribe, is his 'ami'—even though the
nomads are historically the enemies of the oasis-dwellers. So when

Ibrahim dies, Idriss is faced with utter solitude: 'La mort tragique d'Ibrahim avait ouvert un grand vide d'amitié autour de lui que pas un garçon de l'oasis ne pouvait remplir' (28). His search for his photograph will consequently involve a quest for human contact, for kindred souls, although this contact will rarely be erotic—when he showers with the young goldsmith on the car ferry, for instance, 'la terrible solitude dont il souffrait corps et âme' is relieved by ' [leur] contact physique', which is in no way genitally sexual (102).

Above all, Idriss is marginalised by the fact that he is neither wholly oasian nor wholly nomadic: he is drawn to both traditions, yet cannot fully adhere to either. The novel's opening sentence makes this point symbolically, revealing that his flock consists of both sheep and goats, the sheep being essentially docile or sedentary, the goats being 'toujours prêtes à s'égailler dans les éboulis', or nomadic. As Ibrahim dances on the crossbeam of the well, he shows his penis to Idriss, taunting him: 'Oh, queue ronde! Regarde! Moi, j'ai la queue pointue!' (20). Another apparently gratuitous detail, this is much more than adolescent teasing, for Ibrahim is suggesting to Idriss that because he himself is not circumcised, he is freer than Idriss: in Tabelbala, boys are circumcised between the ages of three years and eleven years, not as an initiation or rite of passage, but as a sign of their affiliation to Islam. Idriss is therefore physically marked as irrevocably different from his best friend: he belongs to one culture, Ibrahim to another, and his religious scarring will always separate them.

However, in the oasis itself, Idriss has been designated as different since his infancy. Before he was born, his mother had two stillborn children, so according to Talbelbala custom he was 'vendu aux nègres' (25) and until the age of six years brought up and dressed as a 'negro', his head shaven, with only a single crest of hair running from his forehead to the back of his neck (26). Thus, while one part of his body bears a mark of belonging (circumcision), another part bore, during his formative years, a mark of his non-belonging—albeit as a way of protecting him against malevolent fate.

In the first chapters, Idriss is systematically defined as not only marginal but also as fragmented—thereby prefiguring the kaleidoscopic nature of his experiences on his way to Paris and the place Vendôme. Tournier's choice of Tabelbala as Idriss's native village was inspired, for it is one of the most isolated oases in the Western Sahara—where even today the inhabitants speak their own language (kora n-die). The population is mainly Belbali and the text tells us that Idriss is imbued with the Belbali mentality (24-5), but Tournier also repeatedly defines him as a Berber. This specification is crucial (if, it must be said, somewhat recondite), for the Berbers vehemently proclaim their difference from other North African Arab peoples and, significantly, the Berbers are fairly recent immigrants into Tabelbala. By immigrating to France, Idriss is therefore both 'betraying' his family and home and repeating the history of his people!

Tournier considers the opposition between nomad and sedentary to be one of the fundamental structuring myths of our culture. In almost all of his works, he rewrites the Genesis legend of Creation, paying particular attention to the struggle between Cain (the sedentary cultivator of his garden) and Abel (the ever-eager nomad and hunter). As we all know, Cain killed his brother out of jealousy and, in His anger, God set a mark upon him which both protected him and condemned him to a nomadic life (see *Genesis,* IV: 1-16). Tournier consistently privileges the true, self-chosen nomad, whilst also recognising the value of staying at home. He himself makes several international trips every year, but each time he suffers from the 'angoisse' of leaving his house and garden. Perhaps the best definition of him as a human being and as a writer is that given in the title of his collection of autobiographical and aesthetico-philosophical musings: *Le Vagabond immobile* (1984).

Idriss is an alter ego for his creator. More than any other of Tournier's protagonists, he incarnates his creator—first, as a character caught between the desire to stay at home and the need to leave and travel, and second, as a figure of Tournier's own ambivalent responses to the very different processes of the naïve reading of information and the 'sophisticated' literary reading of texts.

By making Idriss a passive receptor of visual and verbal texts, Tournier appears to rewrite in novelistic terms his oft-repeated statement that he himself has no creative imagination and is dependent on his researches for his plots and imagery. Readers, though, cannot but see this statement as ironic, because of the way in which his narration is articulated. Idriss may aspire to be a nomad; the reader is textually obliged to wander in a different way, in order to achieve a liberation from the tyranny of others' discourses. In other words, the presentation of Idriss's passivity demands the active intervention of the reader—who will ensure the metamorphosis of Idriss from simpleton to hero.

Tournier is, no doubt, playfully disingenuous in his many novelistic and metacritical justifications of naïvety. His texts are so erudite and intertextually complex that alert readers cannot but recognise that their semantic functioning contests any global authorial statement, and that all apparently episodic details need to be scrutinised for both their intratextual and their extratextual meanings.

One significant example of this play is the name of the young protagonist Idriss. In a series of interviews in the late 1980s, Tournier explained that he chose the name because it is a common name in Tabelbala and on the frontiers of Algeria and Morocco—and, furthermore, one which (for him at least) has an 'Oriental' sonority. Critics have tended to believe all Tournier's statements (perhaps because he is such a seductively convincing explainer of his own work!), with the result that they omitted to follow up the clues to subversion that he provides within the novel.

The novel presents us fleetingly with another Idriss whose fate is not unrelated to that of our young Berber shepherd. Intervening once more into a superficially objective recording of events, the narrator arrogates the right to tell us of how in 1969 Oum Kalsoum's concert in Benghazi delayed the coup which would finally overthrow King Idriss of Libya (194). A clever play on verifiable contemporary history as a means to counterpoint the novel's fictions, this intervention serves to remind the reader that nothing can be read in a monovalent way. And there is more.

Readers of Tournier's work know that he is almost obsessively fascinated by etymology and that every proper name is chosen for its culturally illuminating (and provocative) connotations. 'Idriss' may well be a common name in North Africa; it is also, in a diluted or amputated form, the name of a ginger beer sold in cans throughout the Western world (*Idris*). Given the novel's amusedly ironic assault on brand names (*Palmeraie* for *Oasis, Soleil* for *Lux,* etc), the reader might be satisfied with the above explanations of the protagonist's name. Yet given Tournier's mischievous delight in onomastic play, we must look further. The Arabic root of Idriss (which is normally transliterated as *dars*) gives to this name two meanings: he who effaces or obliterates, and he who learns from experience. The first meaning will find its full force at the end of the novel, but the second is closer to Tournier's pedagogical impulses. In 'La Condition de romancier', his introduction to a 1989 edition of his first three novels, he criticises the paucity of the French language which uses the one word *expérience* to designate two very different mental openings onto the external world.[1] Brought up by parents who were both Germanists, and trained as a philosopher, he prefers the distinction made in German between *Experiment,* or the deliberate causation of some phenomenon in order to study it scientifically and *Erfahrung,* which means literally the accumulated knowledge acquired as one travels. He insists that *Erfahrung*-type experience is essential to all forms of writing and especially to the creation of novels, and his protagonists usually themselves engage in writing—until Gilles de Rais in *Gilles & Jeanne* and Idriss in *La Goutte d'or!* This is undoubtedly because the former left no diaries and Tournier was determined to invent no written documents to 'justify' his

---

[1] Michel Tournier, *Vendredi ou les limbes du Pacifique; Le Roi des aulnes; Les Météores* (Gallimard, collection 'Biblos', 1989), pp. vii-xx. A first version of this essay was written for *Paragraph: A Journal of Critical Theory,* 10 (1987), pp. 1-3 (tr. Ninette Bailey and Michael Worton).

recuperative reading of Gilles's life, and because the latter must, for the
purposes of the novel, remain unable to write or read—until he meets
Abd Al Ghafari and is initiated into the Arabic tradition of calligraphy.
    Abd Al Ghafari is the last in a series of mentors for Idriss—and the
most liberating. I shall later consider the centrality to the novel of the
lessons of calligraphy, but it seems appropriate here to consider whether
La Goutte d'or does actually conform to the model of the
Bildungsroman, or novel of formation or apprenticeship. Created in
Germany in the eighteenth century, the *Bildungsroman* focuses on one
central character and his or her quest for identity within the context of a
defined social order (usually bourgeois society). The prototype is
Goethe's *Wilhelm Meisters Lehrjahre* (1796), which was followed by his
Wilhelm Meisters Wanderjahre (1829). The true *Bildungsroman* shows
how an artistic temperament can ultimately come to terms with the
demands of social life and its plot has much in common with the quest
story that characterises most myths and fairy tales—with the difference
that the major antagonist is contemporary society. The protagonist is
presented as seeking an accommodation to the dominant ideology that
surrounds him or her, and the narration tends to suggest that such a
resolution is possible. In other words, the author/narrator arrogates the
right to be didactic and to make socio-moral points at the expense of an
invented, naïve hero who will finally (be made to) reintegrate with
society as a mature and economically secure adult.
    Tournier is a great admirer both of Goethe and of Thomas Mann
(whose novella *Tonio Kröger* is a modern example of the genre). Over
the last two decades, he has also repeatedly made public his enduring
unhappiness at having failed the *agrégation de philosophie,* which would
have permitted him to teach in *lycées* and universities. He may well be
speaking tongue in cheek when he says he would rather be a secondary
school teacher than an internationally respected novelist, but there is no
doubting his commitment to pedagogy and indeed all his fictions have a
didactic purpose—it is also appropriate to remember that Tournier
greatly admires Rousseau's *Émile,* another form of the educational
novel. However, although embedded in the *Bildungsroman* tradition,
La Goutte d'or articulates and enacts the novelist's conviction that this
genre has a fascinating past rather than a creatively prospective future.
    All novels of formation and all didactic texts presuppose that the
narrator-novelist is in a position of influence and superiority. Tournier
had previously revelled and excelled in these genres, imposing his
controlling authority through a variety of narrative interventions such
as quotations, epigraphs, and footnotes. In *Le Vent Paraclet,* he also
supplemented his explanations of the genesis of his first three novels
with directives as to how to understand them. However, in *La Goutte
d'or,* he challenges the very authority he had previously arrogated by

offering a kaleidoscopic range of mentors for Idriss. This results in a transfer of interpretative power from the author to the reader—who must actively recognise that such a ceding of authority entails a new mode of readerly responsibility. In the programmatic introduction to his volume of literary essays *Le Vol du vampire*, Tournier radically revised his earlier 'terroristic' position, insisting on the inevitability of the reader's co-creativity and, more significantly, on the desirability of this participation. *Gilles & Jeanne* bears few obvious marks of this change of position, but *La Goutte d'or* is a novel which, in its willed fragmentation, testifies forcefully to the novelist's conversion.

The great triumph of Idriss is not so much that he rediscovers his ethnic and cultural roots but that, by becoming *sourd et aveugle,* he places himself irrevocably outside the structure of French society. Presented with the seductions of earning money and prestige by allowing his image to be disseminated in films or shop-window dummies, he refuses the entire concept of 'climbing the ladder' which underpins contemporary Western capitalist and imagistic society. Crucially, though, Idriss has learned nothing! His discovery of selfhood is an emotional response to his solitude, a function of his nostalgia when the sight of 'his' golden droplet in a jeweller's window opens the floodgates of memory. He triumphs over the society that oppresses him—but the narration deliberately holds back from according to him any political awareness. While some identification with Idriss is necessary if one is to read the novel properly, it is undeniable that the reader is programmed to read between the lines and to recognise that the novel is a critique both of modern French society and of the European literary tradition of the *Bildungsroman.*

In the last chapter, Idriss is reminded by his cousin Achour that he is just another 'bicot' but that, by giving immigrants the most menial of jobs, French society has also given them the means—and the authority—to 'casse[r] tout' (**217**)! This paradox is at the heart of the novel as a story—and as an allegory of reading. What is important is that Idriss does not understand and that from then onwards he remains silent. It is finally time, the text suggests, that the reader engage in the business of interpretation and co-creation. Unlike the traditional *Bildungsroman* hero, Idriss has many, too many mentors, most of whom are themselves bound by the limitations of their specific situations and hence are suspect masters. He himself is a blank slate on which many messages may be written, each one effacing the previous one, each one accepted passively by Idriss who knows only that he wants to 'aller rejoindre ma photo' (**99**). The word 'rejoindre', which is explicitly preferred by Idriss to 'chercher', is a hermeneutic key. It can variously mean to get back to something or someone, to bring back together people or things, to agree with someone's opinion, to catch up with someone and to

resemble somebody's image of one. If one constant relates these
different meanings, it is that of reunion. Idriss is seeking desperately,
innocently, to meet up with his photographic image: such is the plot of
the novel, yet in a text which self-consciously plays with the French
lexicon and with connotations, the choice of the word *rejoindre* has a
structural as well as a semantic function. Idriss's maternal tongue is not
French, so to accord him a fleeting linguistic sophistication amounts to a
crucial authorial intervention whereby Tournier invites the reader to a
hermeneutic dance—in which the reader will always lead.

Idriss has consistently been led by others until he meets the
calligrapher Abd Al Ghafari, who opens for him a door onto the past
and the future and, more importantly, offers a perspective of autonomy:

> Dès sa première calligraphie, Idriss se retrouva plongé dans le temps
> démesuré où il avait vécu sans le savoir à Tabelbala. Il comprenait
> maintenant que ces vastes plages de durée étaient un don de son enfance, et
> qu'il les retrouverait désormais par l'étude, l'exercice et le désintéressement.
> D'ailleurs la faculté offerte au calligraphe d'allonger horizontalement
> certaines lettres introduit dans la ligne des silences, des zones de calme et de
> repos, qui sont le désert même. (**199**)

There is, of course, a problem here, in that the narrator equates the
desert with silence, calm and rest (a rewriting of the 'mer de sable'
metaphor that puzzles and seduces Idriss [**72-3**]). Consonant with the
French literary tradition of Orientalism, this definition is nonetheless
contradicted by all that we learn about the desert in the first chapters of
the novel. The narration may inscribe itself into the very system of
French colonialist fantasy that it seeks to repudiate, but it does this
deliberately in order to highlight the importance of different forms of
writing and reading.

Even in North Africa, Idriss is presented by a series of European
images of his home territory ('ce Sahara empaillé'—**79**), and Mustapha,
the Béchar photographer who fleeces French tourists by photographing
them in front of painted backcloths, offers an aesthetic justification of
his trade which slides into a reinforcing of European attitudes:

> Chaque chose est transcendée par sa représentation en image. Transcendée,
> oui, c'est bien ça. Le Sahara représenté sur cette toile, c'est le Sahara
> idéalisé, et en même temps possédé par l'artiste. (**84**)

The Sahara, says the text, can really be known only by those who live
there, especially as their culture is oral rather than literary and so must
always ultimately remain unknowable by Europeans—even if this very
foreignness calls up and makes possible an infinity of psychosocial
projections, all of which will involve some form of idealisation. The
various explicit textual inscriptions of the concept of idealisation are by

no means innocent, since the novel itself is consciously engaged in a ludic arabesque, plotting the reader's movements and then subverting the authority of this choreography.

Idriss is undoubtedly like Voltaire's Candide; he is innocent, but he is neither pure nor idealised. However, a first (superficial) reading of *La Goutte d'or* might take too seriously the apparent privileging of the Islamic sign over the European image. While Islamic 'wisdom' may be systematically preferred to modern European spectaculism which is presented as irredeemably spoliatory, the text takes care episodically to remind the reader of the dangers of believing anyone or anything.

This is why the calligraphy lesson episode and 'La Reine blonde' are crucial. Abd Al Ghafari is Idriss's first disinterested teacher, and the way in which he imparts to the young Berber the heritage of Arabic culture plays a determining role in the transfer of interpretive power from author to reader. He reveals that every picture is potentially a palimpsest for the calligrapher who can, by drawing letter-signs, transcend the opposition between language and image and thereby offer access to a new mode of representing the world. Tournier's previous novels (notably *Le Roi des aulnes*) insist on the ontological importance of decoding signs and sign-systems; in other words, they articulate and promote a belief in the existence of a single, founding meaning for every event. In his view, the Western metaphysical tradition from Plato and Aristotle onwards indeed legitimises such an approach, whereas Islam privileges the abstract sign and so, like all Oriental and Indian cultural systems, promotes multiplicity of meaning:

> L'image est verrou, l'idole prison, la figure serrure. Une seule clef peut faire tomber ces chaînes: le signe. L'image est toujours rétrospective. C'est un miroir tourné vers le passé. (**201**)

While Tournier's philosophical training was firmly European, over the past decade he has become increasingly fascinated by the Eastern tradition of the *conte* (notably *The Arabian Nights*) and by Eastern painting and aesthetics; hence the attraction of the calligram, which, as Foucault points out, aspires playfully to efface the oldest oppositions of our alphabetical civilisations: to show and to name; to reproduce and to articulate; to look and to read.[2] Tournier's predilection was previously for figurative art, and especially for portraiture, but in his preface to *Hassan Massoudy calligraphe,* he reveals a radical change of position:

> Il conviendrait [...] d'effacer la distinction entre peinture figurative et peinture abstraite, en disant qu'il n'y a de peinture qu'abstraite, mais qu'une partie de la peinture abstraite se cache sous un masque figuratif. Reste que ce masque figuratif empêche en grande partie de voir le visage abstrait, et qu'aux yeux de nombre de spectateurs, il se substitue à lui.

---

[2] See Michel Foucault, *Ceci n'est pas une pipe* (Montpellier: Éditions Fata Morgana, 1973), ch. 2.

> Ce contresens, la calligraphie le rend impossible. Il y a entre le sens de la phrase et la figure calligraphique une relation profonde certes, mais de nature spirituelle et non pas matérielle. Cette relation n'est pas la chaîne d'un esclave, mais le libre feu du lecteur inspiré. L'image, avec tout ce qu'elle a de pesamment contraignant pour l'esprit, se trouve exorcisée par la calligraphie. [...] La lettrine—ornée, frisée, chantournée—qui inaugure le premier mot de chaque chapitre [d'un roman], c'est déjà l'exaltation du signe. C'est le signe abstrait épanoui comme une fleur, comme une rosace. La calligraphie célèbre la liberté de l'esprit.[3]

Calligraphy, in the sense in which it is used in Idriss's crucial encounter with Abd Al Ghafari and in the story 'La Reine blonde', has little to do with its usual meaning in the Western world (the art of writing beautifully). A powerful example of how a foreign cultural tradition can creatively invade or 'immigrate into' the European consciousness, the calligram augments the alphabet and it repeats something without the aid of verbal rhetoric. In some ways, it is tautological, since it shows what it says. However, while rhetoric revels in the possibilities of language, repeating the same thing in different words or using one word to say several things,[4] the calligram's doubleness operates an excavation of the visual referent of language in order to remind us that the absence which haunts all discourse can be transformed into presence—provided that the reader-spectator recognises that nothing is single. Hassan Massoudy makes this clear:

> Il existe une infinité de traductions calligraphiques pour un même mot ou une même phrase. On obtiendra un graphisme totalement différent sans aucun rapport entre eux, si ce n'est leur signification. [...] Cette diversité est possible grâce aux divers styles et aux variantes propres à chaque style et aussi grâce, bien sûr, aux diverses interprétations et possibilités créatrices. (*HMC*, 91)

In his book, Hassan Massoudy includes, amongst many discrete calligrams, several variations on a theme: three calligrams of Buddha's statement 'Que l'homme surmonte la colère par l'amour (*HMC*, 54), three calligrams of the French colloquialism 'Parlons peu mais parlons bien' (*HMC*, 66-7), and twelve calligrams of 'La paix' (*HMC*, 90 and 112), all of which are greatly different from each other. If there is no single visual incarnation of a verbal text, suggests the calligrapher's art, then that text must be and must remain in a constant state of flux—and so it will constantly demand rereadings and re-evaluations.

---

[3] Michel Tournier, 'Préface', in H. Massoudy, *Hassan Massoudy calligraphe* (Flammarion, 1986), p. 3. Further references to this book are given in the text, with the page numbers preceded by the abbreviation *HMC*.

[4] In 'La Reine blonde', the calligrapher Ibn Al Houdaïda reveals to Riad that *figure* can mean variously *visage humain, figure de diction, figure de construction, figure de mots [trope], figure de pensée*, and... *signe calligraphique* (**209**). The text thus reminds us of the power of rhetoric in order precisely to undermine it.

La Goutte d'or has been described by its author as offering an antidote to the pathological Western obsession with images, mirrors and reflections. On the narrative level, this antidote is the Islamic sign which refuses to be representative or mimetic; on the narratological level, the antidote is the creative (and interrogative) activity of reading.

One of the most fertile 'logical' slippages in the novel is the attribution to Arab characters of a 'European' concern with reading as decoding. For instance, in 'La Reine blonde', Ibn Al Houdaïda explains to Riad:

> L'image est douée d'un rayonnement paralysant, telle la tête de Méduse qui changeait en pierre tous ceux qui croisaient son regard. Pourtant cette fascination n'est irrésistible qu'aux yeux des analphabètes. En effet l'image n'est qu'un enchevêtrement de signes [...]. Pour le lettré, l'image n'est pas muette. Son rugissement de fauve se dénoue en paroles nombreuses et gracieuses. Il n'est que de savoir lire...
> Dès lors Riad apprit à lire. (**208-209**)

The essential problem for Idriss is that he is between cultures and, moreover, that he is untrained in reading signs: he has always trusted the surface of what he sees without recognising that all signs, however 'abstract' they may seem, are inhabited by hidden meanings. The reference to Medusa is by no means innocent. It alerts the reader (yet again!) to the fact that this novel is written by a European for Europeans, since there is no equivalent myth in Islamic culture. Nevertheless, the significance is patent: the image *petrifies,* functions as a castrating force, and denies the possibility of freedom. The only true liberation is to be found not through an abolition of images but through a radically new, revolutionary way of reading the images that surround and enchain us.

What is particularly seductive for Tournier in the Oriental tradition of calligraphy is the explicit insistence on the role of the body in the act of calligraphy. He inserts into the novel Hassan Massoudy's strictures on the importance of breathing properly and goes on to stress the crucial function of the right hand, 'l'organe le plus spiritualisé du corps' (**202**). Calligraphy is presented to Idriss as a means of recuperating his ethno-cultural past; more vitally, it will become for him, as for Riad, a means of healing the wounds inflicted by blond women—by learning how to rewrite them, that is to say, by inscribing them as multiple into the script of his life.

In 'Orphée noir', his introduction to Senghor's *Anthologie de la nouvelle poésie nègre et malgache,* Sartre states that 'il s'agit [...] pour le noir de mourir à la culture blanche pour renaître à l'âme noire [...], il s'agit [...] de devenir ce qu'il est'.[5] An initial, if now somewhat

[5] Jean-Paul Sartre, 'Orphée noir', in L.S. Senghor, *Anthologie de la nouvelle poésie nègre et malgache* (Presses Universitaires de France, 1948), p. xxiii.

recalcitrant disciple of Sartre, Tournier would agree with this existentialist programme, but *La Goutte d'or* articulates a more complex position. On the narrative level, it affirms the necessity of establishing identity, especially as an immigrant; on the narratological level, it incorporates Idriss into an interrogation of the ways in which we live and read in French society. And the novel incessantly challenges every attitude which it seems to present as privileged.

Idriss is created as a young protagonist desperately seeking knowledge. He is also 'set up' as someone who is naïve, ignorant of what is real in everything around him. If we read *La Goutte d'or* merely as a novel of formation, we miss the point, for Idriss is used, used as a trope: his cultural blindness and deafness serve pedagogically as images of our own societal and personal failings. His major fictional precursors (Robinson, Abel Tiffauges, Alexandre, Gilles de Rais) are all granted a sexuality which they either embrace or reject in order to establish a sense of their being, but Idriss is confronted by scenes and events in which gender is ambiguous. Significantly, though, most of these ambiguities are indicated to the reader, while Idriss himself remains unaware of the implications.

A first example occurs in the first chapter when the she-camel has fallen down the well and an old male camel comes to lick the orphaned colt:

> Il était peu probable que le vieux mâle cédât à une soudaine vocation paternelle. Il devait plutôt apprécier sur le corps tremblant et humide du petit l'odeur violente de la mère. Quant au chamelon, perdu d'esseulement, il se serrait contre ce protecteur inespéré, puis emporté par l'instinct, il fouillait du museau ses génitoires à la recherche d'hypothétiques mamelles. (**19**)

Deprived of its mother, the colt loses its sense of gender difference. This is a frequent occurrence for suddenly-orphaned animals, so neither Idriss nor the reader could or should be surprised. However, as the text progresses, it accumulates details of Idriss's marginality, gradually making clear that he too is, in his own way, orphaned, cut off from his past. His father is absent from the text (he is mentioned only indirectly in the form 'ses parents'—**28**), and, like all children in Tabelbala, Idriss was deliberately neglected when he was a baby and left dirty by his mother, who wanted to protect him from the evil eye. Although he has male mentors in Ibrahim and his uncle Mogadem, both are outsiders: Ibrahim because he is a nomadic Chaamba, Mogadem because he is 'un solitaire' who had always refused to marry and is consequently considered in the oasis to be 'un marginal' (**53**). Interestingly, with the exception of these and of the calligraphers (both real and fictional) and, to a lesser extent, the young goldsmith and Idriss's cousin, Achour, most of of Idriss's knowledge of Arab culture comes to him through women:

his grandmother, his mother, their neighbour, Kuka, Zett Zobeida, Oum Kalsoum—and Kerstine in 'Barberousse'. Kerstine may be only a character in a folk tale, but her explanation to Kheir ed Dîn/ Barberousse of the reparative miracle of her tapestry is crucial for Idriss and for the reader: «Ce qu'a fait une femme, seules les mains d'une femme peuvent le défaire» (46).

Life in the oasis is devoted to the cultivation of the earth—which is conceived as the maternal element. A force that demands total obedience to her laws, the earth is, however, a harsh mistress who punishes those who dare to challenge her, be it by seeking to live out their desires independently or by seeking to recover from her what she has taken. The inhabitants of the oasis acquiesce docilely, like Idriss's sheep, whereas he himself would also like to 's'égailler'—like his goats. This ambivalence is underlined by his affection for the nomad Ibrahim, who has been 'rendu un peu fou par le soleil et la solitude' (11) and who contravenes religious laws:

> Son impiété épouvantait souvent Idriss. Il n'hésitait pas à boire debout, en tenant la jatte d'une seule main, alors qu'il faut, quand on boit, avoir au moins un genou à terre et serrer le récipient à deux mains. (*ibid.* see also **78**)

Ibrahim is attractive to Idriss precisely because he is transgressive, daring to contest the authority of all laws—and because he reminds Idriss of the need to establish an autonomous identity and to sexualise himself *against* and *within* a matriarchal culture.

The novel presents Arab culture as fundamentally maternal (and matriarchal). Zett Zobeida the dancer and Oum Kalsoum the singer, who are superficially very different, are accorded identical epithets, culminating in the problematically paradoxical tripartite definition of Oum Kalsoum as 'épouse', 'madone' and 'vestale' (192). One cannot deny that this reading of the workings of Arab culture is partial—and indeed several Arab readers wrote to Tournier to complain that he had 'emasculated' Islam. Nevertheless, the insistence on women's roles is essential for the novel's interrogation of quests for identity, in that it enables Tournier to create a context which confuses Idriss.

An adolescent of fifteen years of age, Idriss is in yet another way marginal, being between childhood and adulthood and uncertain of what sexuality or gender mean. The laws of Belbali society consider him to be an adult, and so exclude him from being present at intimate ceremonies and discussions between women—yet after Ibrahim's death, he has nowhere to go to find friendship or instruction. So he stays 'illicitly' at home and overhears a dialogue between his mother and Kuka:

> Idriss se faisait oublier, comme il avait appris à le faire chaque fois que,
> dans la demeure trop exiguë, il assistait à une scène dont il était en principe
> exclu en raison de son âge ou de son sexe. (**26**)

Segregation or exclusion is the rule in the oasis. What, then, can a
young man do to establish himself as a sexed and gendered person?
Idriss may well look forward to the wedding of Aïcha ben Baada, a girl
of his age; once there, he realises that 'cette grosse fille passive et molle
était dépourvue de mystère et de prestige' (**28**). Even her wedding-day
beauty has been created by the application of products like henna,
myrtle, incense, walnut bark, cloves and wild iris rhizomes (**27**). She is
herself 'sans charmes' (**28**), but she and her family have 'captured' her
husband who is henceforth condemned to 's'enraciner solennellement' in
Tabelbala (*ibid.*). For Idriss, women as wives and mothers are
imprisoning forces:

> Partir. [...] C'était la poussée d'un vieil atavisme nomade qui ne
> s'accommodait pas d'un avenir enraciné dans les lieux de sa naissance, de la
> prison mouvante, chaleureuse mais d'autant plus redoutable, que forment
> autour d'un homme, une femme et des enfants. Non, il était décidé à ne pas
> se marier. (**57**)

He has to escape in order to liberate himself from the maternal forces
that surround him, yet even Mogadem assumes that Idriss will
eventually be drawn back to the oasis where, as an adult, he will be able
to decide whether or not to conform to the laws of the matriarchy. He
urges him:

> —Va chercher ta photo, rapporte-la ici, et cloue-la au mur de ta chambre,
> comme la mienne ici. C'est mieux comme ça. Ensuite tu pourras te marier et
> avoir des enfants. À moins que tu préfères rester seul comme moi. (**59**)

As a model and as an adviser, Mogadem offers a transgressive
alternative to the familial ideology of Tabelbala, but Idriss cannot fully
follow his advice, since he has yet to understand and internalise sexual
difference. He remains a child throughout the novel in the sense that he
never metaphorically severs the umbilical cord and this is because he
does not know what (his) sexuality is and so cannot assume it. The title
of the novel refers mainly to the golden droplet lost by Zett Zobeida,
picked up by Idriss, stolen by the Marseille prostitute and finally seen
again by Idriss in the jeweller's window in the Place Vendôme. As we
have seen, early in the text, the narrator posits this jewel as
characteristic of the anti-representational culture of Islam: 'A l'opposé
des pendeloques qui imitent le ciel, la terre, les animaux du désert et les
poissons de la mer, la bulle dorée ne veut rien dire qu'elle-même. C'est
le signe pur, la forme absolue' (**31**).
     The reader may be programmed by some textual directives and by

Tournier's many statements in interviews to read the story only as an assault on the Western obsession with the semantic implications of images; however s/he is also offered a historical explanation of the meaning of the droplet which contests the notion that 'la goutte d'or' is just an abstract sign:

> C'est un insigne romain et même étrusque qui subsiste encore de nos jours dans certaines tribus sahariennes. Les enfants romains de naissance libre portaient cette goutte d'or suspendue à leur cou par une bélière, comme preuve de leur condition. Lorsqu'ils changeaient la robe prétexte contre la toge virile, ils abandonnaient également la bulla aurea en offrande aux lares domestiques. (103)

On the diegetic or narrative level, this explanation lends support to interpretations which see *La Goutte d'or* only as a novel of formation or initiation: Idriss 'becomes a man' when he sleeps with the Marseille prostitute and so has no further need of the droplet as a witness to his youth or 'innocence'. He has entered the world of men. It is perhaps appropriate to mention in passing that black theorists and activists, such as James Baldwin and Frantz Fanon, have pointed out that the first thing many coloured male immigrants do on arriving in Europe is to go to a brothel to have sex with a white (and preferably blonde) woman. In other words, many immigrants see sex *qua* exploitative domination as a condition of social integration.

But... Idriss is picked up by the prostitute rather than seeking her out, and she steals his golden droplet. Consequently, he remains in the double position of victim and child: he is passive—'Docilement' (**110**)—and when he tries to take back his *gri-gri,* his hand is 'timide' (**111**): though genitally sexed and societally coded as male, he has neither the knowledge nor the desire to act out the role of the 'virile', 'masterful' man.

Despite what the young goldsmith says, Idriss, of course, is not really 'libre', for he is born the prisoner of a cultural system, and he loses the droplet through a theft, not as an offering to the *lares* or tutelary deities of a home. The young goldsmith's explanation thus has a subversive textual function, alerting the reader to the importance of transcultural references. In ancient Rome, the shedding of the golden droplet was a rite of passage, yet it also involved a show of deference to the *lares,* whereas Idriss precisely wishes to escape the laws of the (matriarchal) household and to refuse to be manoeuvred into marriage by his parents (see **28**). The term ''libre' is therefore reconsidered. For the Romans, when the free-born boy becomes a man, he actually loses his individual freedom and commits himself to laws of domesticity; for Idriss, the loss of the droplet means a (temporary) liberation from the laws of the oasis.

The novel is networked by semantic ambiguities such as this (other examples relevant to 'libre' are 'nubile' (28) and 'esclave' (168). All of Tournier's work is marked by his fascination with etymology and lexical ambiguity; it is also haunted by explorations of 'marginal' sexualities. For Tournier, sexuality is a political issue. But it is also a domain of human experience which must be (re-)individualised and incorporated into our ontological and metaphysical meditations; we must, suggests Tournier, live out our personal sexuality in the knowledge that erotic experience can provide us with keys which may open doors onto a viable sense of our *Dasein* or being-in-the-world. His fictions may well repeatedly propose that non-genital sexuality is the ultimate goal, yet this form of transcendence or sublimation is possible only once we are authentically sexualised. And Idriss fails in this—because his models are ambiguous.

For instance, when he meets the Marseille prostitute who reminds him of the originator of his quest, it transpires that his primary and primal encounter has been with an androgynous figure:

> Idriss était ébloui par les épaules nues et grasses de la fille. La femme de la Land Rover avait une chemisette qui lui donnait un air vaguement masculin (**110**)

His last partner, the pneumatic drill, is itself androgynous. Achour tells him: 'Le marteau-piqueur, c'est épatant, tu peux me croire. C'est ton zob, tu comprends? Un zob géant. Avec ça, tu crèves Paris, tu niques la France!' (**218**). The terms of this statement merit serious consideration, for they represent a highly sexualised displacement of the immigrant's desire to gain antagonistic power by sleeping with a blond European woman. A *zob,* or cock, evokes aggressive heterosexual virility, but also reminds us of le grand Zob, the homosexual pimp; 'crever' means to burst, but is also used in erotic slang to mean 'to fuck someone's brains out'; 'niquer' may initially have meant to thumb one's nose at someone but its current slang meaning is 'to fuck'. These three terms are each double, and each is employed exclusively by men who use women as the objects of their desire. To accept these terms would mean for Idriss that he had become a 'man', an angry exploiter of women. Thankfully, the novel ends with a reversal of this reprehensible sexism. The pneumatic drill is gendered as female: 'C'était sa danseuse, sa cavalière infernale, Zett Zobeida métamorphosée en robot enragé' (**220**).

However, even this salutary reversal is textually complex, since the feminine, though now privileged, is also presented as mechanical and out of control ('ce robot enragé'). Idriss, like Frédéric Moreau in Flaubert's *L'Éducation sentimentale,* has learned nothing about emotional and sexual relations, but both serve as anti-models for the reader who will—or should!—learn from the lessons they fail to learn.

Idriss's quest is not for sexual fulfilment; it is for someone or something to fill the emotional gaps in his life. Apart from the Marseille encounter, Idriss has no sexual experience. While his major problem may be his wish to find himself, his desire is always-already castrated by the ways in which sexuality is determined, appropriated and negated by the matriarchal system of the oasis. So Idriss's desire can and indeed must be seen as a functional displacement: he wants to find his photographic image in order to abolish its power as a (foreign) supplement to his existence, and he also needs to release himself from the chains of all cultural projections.

Like many adolescents, he and Ibrahim have fun comparing their penises, but when Ibrahim flaunts his before falling into the well, this is not to show that it is bigger but to remind Idriss of their cultural difference, in that only Idriss has been circumcised (**20**). When, on the car-ferry, Idriss takes a shower with the goldsmith, the two boys have to cling together in 'une cellule de douche minuscule' (**102**): the term 'cellule' is crucial, for it reminds us of Tournier's concern with twins and genetic cells in *Les Météores*. Neither of these events is homo-erotic, and the narrator is at pains to conflate maternalism and eroticism, thereby neutralising the latter:

> La tendresse maternelle et l'érotisme des amants ne sont que des aspects particuliers de l'ardent besoin de contact physique qui fait le fond de la chair et du cœur. (*ibid.*)

Later on, Idriss is confronted by other modes of displaced sexuality (for instance, Zob and his gang of rent-boys and Milan with his dummies), yet when he talks with Achille Mage, he is offered a proposal which, though partially couched in sexual terms, corresponds to his own desire for human warmth:

> Écoute-moi bien, Idriss de mon cœur, Idriss de mon cul. Toi t'es un pauvre clochard [..]. Moi je suis riche et puissant. [..] Mais la vraie vérité, c'est que moi aussi je suis un pauvre clochard, et j'ai besoin de toi. J'ai besoin de toi, tu m'entends? [...] Pour quoi faire, pour quoi faire! [...] Pour *vivre*, nom de Dieu! (**142-3**; my emphasis)

Eternally 'sourd et aveugle', Idriss does not recognise this invitation for what it is: it is no attempt at seduction, but an appeal for friendship, for a bonding. Eve Kosofsky Sedgwick has argued convincingly that, in Western patriarchal society, male behaviour has always existed as a continuum. She coins the term 'homosociality' and proposes that homosexuality is merely an extreme form of male bonding.[6] From his first novel, *Vendredi,* until such recent texts as 'Blandine ou la visite du père' and 'Aventures africaines', in *Le Médianoche amoureux,* Tournier has been consistent in challenging sex and gender stereotypes, notably those imposed on men. However, in *La Goutte d'or,* Idriss's only sexual act is not described. This is because the genital sexuality involved is not important: what matters is the fact that the prostitute is just another link in the chain of women in Idriss's history.

Zett Zobeida, who is black and a female version of the 'nègres' to whom Idriss was 'sold', is an outsider, albeit one who is invited to represent the 'âme' of the wedding celebrations (**29-30**). She is largely responsible for his departure; she is also the person who, as the major figure of nostalgic fantasy, makes possible the beginnings of his return to his culture, if not physically to the oasis. But (how) is she a woman? This double question is central to the novel, for Idriss both seeks in every woman the image of 'la femme de la Land Rover' and yet is unable to recognise or accept the full otherness of women or, more precisely, the female.

When the ironically-named Bonami proposes that he should be the model of a series of shop-window dummies, he experiences anxiety at the prospect of once again losing (sight of) his identity by becoming a mere simulacrum:

> Il se voyait multiplié par dix, par cent, réduit à une infinité de poupées de cire figées dans des poses ridicules sous les yeux de la foule massée devant les vitrines de Tati.(**182**)

In much modern critical theory, the term simulacrum is used to mean an image which passes itself off as a reality. It is a copy of a copy—for which there is no original. Tournier has explored this phenomenon in different ways in several of his novels and short stories; in *La Goutte d'or,* he uses it as a way of showing how the image-making processes of the 'société du spectacle' deprive individuals of their uniqueness. Idriss learns painfully that modern European culture is exploitative and that its manipulations reduce being to appearing. However, he is also complicit with these systems of mechanical reproduction, in that he duplicates the 'femme de la Land Rover', seeing her in other women. Part of the reason for this behaviour is Idriss's adolescent inability to distinguish between his wish to establish an individual identity, his need to become fully integrated into the North African cultural collectivity, and the awakening of his sexuality. In Tabelbala, he refused to accept that girls

---

[6] See her *Between Men: English Literature and Male Homosocial Desire* (New York: Columbia University Press, 1985), *passim.* Luce Irigaray has argued, more aggressively, that Western society is founded on and grounded in pederasty; see, for example, *Ce sexe qui n'en est pas un* (Seuil, 1977) and *Éthique de la différence sexuelle* (Minuit, 1984).

of his own age could be desirable, yet, once in France, he is robbed by
the prostitute and his experience at the peep show leaves him 'tremblant
de désir frustré' (163). What he does not realise, but what the reader is
systematically programmed to understand, is that a cultural politics of
mass production restricts the field of desire.

Having seen the 'femme-lionne' from behind a screen, he wants to
meet her—as he wants to encounter his photographic image.
Functioning here somewhat blatantly as the mouthpiece of the author,
Achour warns him against trying to literalise or concretise an image:

> —Tu es fou de vouloir la rencontrer [...]. Cette femme, c'est comme si elle
> n'existait pas! [...] Elle existait pour tes yeux, mais pas pour tes mains. Ici
> tout est pour les yeux, rien pour les mains. Les vitrines, c'est comme le
> cinéma et la télévision, pour les yeux, seulement pour les yeux! C'est des
> choses que tu devrais comprendre. Le plus tôt serait le mieux. (163-4)

The narrator immediately makes clear that 'Idriss n'avait pas encore
compris ces choses, puisque, dès le lendemain, il retournait rue Saint-
Denis' (164)—where he is confronted by a cleaning woman with very
short pepper-and-salt hair, a mask-like face hardened by the absence of
make-up, and varicose veins. A degree of verbal ambiguity leaves the
reader to decide whether or not this was the previous day's star of the
peep-show—'Et [...] sa grande bouche dessina le rictus amer de la lionne
fouettée' (165)—dutifully mopping up the ejaculations of the men who
had believed in her (or, rather, in their own fantasies). If so, as another
example of a simulacrum, she has no reality as an object of desire,
except when she is an actress playing a role.

This episode is important in the story of Idriss's education.
Furthermore, it is the most obvious example of how all images function
pornographically in the 'société du spectacle': they both frustrate and
degrade the viewer by evoking a desire which can never be satisfied
because it is based on an illusion—and they promote libidinal
satisfaction as available only vicariously or as sex-for-sale.

In the novel's sexual scenarios, women are presented as complying
passively with this ideology (even the Marseille prostitute's theft of the
droplet bears witness to her acceptance that she can be bought). The two
most important women for Idriss are Zett Zobeida whose dancing he
watches but whom he does not meet, and Oum Kalsoum whom he does
not see but of whom he is told. They therefore become for him not so
much images of womanhood as symbols of Arabic culture. Zett Zobeida
is 'l'antithèse et peut-être l'antidote de la femme platinée à l'appareil de
photo' (31); she is explicitly associated with the 'pure' sign of the
droplet, which is ' [un] symbole de libération, [l'] antidote de
l'asservissement par l'image' (220). She can consequently be seen as a
virgin figure who offers Idriss escape from the blond French 'whores'

who represent the manipulative 'société du spectacle'. Critics have often
claimed that Tournier's novels are structured on and by a series of
binary oppositions, and, on a first reading, Zett Zobeida may seem to be
a pole in the following oppositions: 'nègre' / 'oasien', black / white,
virgin/whore, woman/man. However, none of these categories is simple
in *La Goutte d'or,* since, for example, Idriss was 'vendu aux nègres', the
blonde woman's hair is dyed, and the male/female dichotomy is
repeatedly challenged.

The text insistently equates Zett Zobeida and Oum Kalsoum. Both
are cultural outsiders, Zett as 'une femme noire' (**29**) and Oum because
'elle a l'audace de refuser l'arabe littéraire et de chanter à la radio en
dialecte égyptien' (**193**); Zett is described as 'cette statue voilée [...,]
cette statue de voile' (**30**), thereby textually replacing Ibrahim ('une
vivante statue'—**20**), while Oum's handkerchief ('voile') is as much a
defining element as the scarf she always wears 'par atavisme arabe'
(**193**)—and indeed, *Kalsoum* means 'étendard', or banner. Both are
associated with weddings which they help to consummate ritually; both
are described in terms of 'l'âme' and 'la flamme' (**30**; **193**).

In textual terms, Zett is undoubtedly the primary and ultimate figure
of woman for Idriss in his (initially unwitting) quest for reintegration
with his culture. Yet, as a marginal, as an outsider, she needs to be
complemented textually by Oum who is equally, if differently,
ambiguous as a woman. Oum began her career 'habillée en garçon'
(**192**) and has ' [une] voix un peu trop grave pour une femme, la voix
[d'un] jeune bédouin' (**196**). She is 'si profondément *enracinée* dans sa
terre deltaïque qu'elle éprouve toujours une certaine répugnance à
s'aventurer dans cet Extrême-Occident que sont les capitales
européennes et les grandes cités américaines' (**195**; my emphasis). Oum
Kalsoum is, of course, a real person as opposed to Zett who is purely
fictional, but the narrator's descriptions of her inscribe her as a
tropological figure into the web of intratextual play: Mohammed
Amouzine explains that, of all the Arab peoples, the Egyptians are the
least nomadic (**191**), so Oum's willingness to travel in order to unify the
Arab communities in Western societies rewrites Idriss's negative
response to 'enracinement' as a generous positivity. Oum may in reality
look a little like Jean-Paul Sartre: 'une grosse dame au visage lourd,
masqué par d'épaisses lunettes noires' (**196**); she is nevertheless
desirable by men as a representation of, or a screen for, their nostalgia:

> Oum Kalsoum a un public presque exclusivement masculin, et c'est une
> femme sans homme. [...] C'est qu'elle se veut l'épouse de tout le peuple
> arabe, une sorte de madone, une vestale de la nation qui vit son art comme
> une mission à la fois sentimentale et patriotique. [...] La foule l'acclame avec
> des mots insensés: «Tu es à nous. Tu es la fiancée de ma vie. Depuis que je
> te connais, je suis sourd, je n'entends que ta voix, je suis muet, je ne parle
> que de toi.»(**192-3**)

This passage may use the term 'insensés' to alert the reader to the need to read sceptically; it also reveals how men exiled from their country and from their cultural identity will invariably seek a symbol of their past, no matter how displaced (while they are deaf and mute, they find through Oum a way of speaking about themselves as individuals as well as about themselves as parts of a collectivity) . This is an acute analysis of sociopolitical realities, but here, as throughout the novel, the societally functional place of women is left ambiguous. Are women no more than objects to be exploited or cultural standard-bearers? When the narrator states that Oum sees herself as wife, madonna and vestal virgin for the Arab community, he is patently equating her role with that of the Virgin Mary in Christian cultures, thereby desexualising her and encouraging the reader to rethink pre-determined definitions of women. Zett as a dancer and as a woman is textually reduced to her 'ventre', which, 'animé d'une vie autonome et intensément expressive', is 'la bouche sans lèvres de tout ce corps, la partie parlante, souriante, grimaçante de tout ce corps' (30). When Idriss listens to the sad, heart-rending recordings of Oum, he 'revoyait alors le ventre luisant et noir de la danseuse, cette bouche sans lèvres par laquelle s'exprimait tout le corps pudiquement voilé' (197). The songs he hears lead to emotional vertigo and are a form of hypnosis, but the narrative links between Zett and Oum lead the reader to focus on the over-determined image of the liberating woman as 'un ventre', which in French is a lexical mark of maternity. The female belly can be perceived as erotic (cf. 'luisant'), yet the main force of the narration is focused on the belly as ' [une] bouche sans lèvres'. This image crucially desexualises the woman. Having refuted the traditional figure of woman as a silent body through the epithet 'parlante'' and having therefore accorded her the possibility to express her own desire, the text deprives her (metaphorical) mouth of its lips. This is certainly not, as some critics have suggested, a reference to the barbaric custom of excision which, still practised in some parts of the African and Islamic worlds, neuters female sexuality, for such excision has no place in Belbali initiatory rituals for girls or young women.

This image is an integral, if subversive, element in the novel's privileging of woman/women as redemptive. Its textual articulation is in no way innocent, since it reveals how women can be—and are— mutilated even by those men who admire them most. The various other references to lips throughout the novel gender them as female. Consequently, to deprive any part of the female body of its lips is to deny femaleness. If Zett's belly is defined by the narrator and remembered by Idriss as a 'bouche sans lèvres', this is because both suppose that symbolic fantasising is the same as physiological knowledge: in all societies, be they phallocentric or matriarchal, the

woman's sexual 'mouth' is, surely, her vulva, not her belly! By
depriving the two determining women of their lips, the male narrating
or responding figures make them mouthpieces of their own fantasies
rather than autonomous, female-gendered individuals. This transfer
onto women's bodies of male fantasies is mainly metaphorical, but the
'femme-lionne' of the peep-show bears the physical scars of her
subservience to a pornographic male culture: 'Elle cambra ses reins et
écarta ses cuisses pour faire bâiller sa vulve rasée de frais...' (**163**). Her
shaven vulva is another form of the 'bouche sans lèvres', one which
denies the bodily reality of adult female sexuality and which,
furthermore, reminds the reader that every image or metaphor must be
read knowingly with suspicion.

The textual presentation of sexuality is carefully crafted in order to
challenge gender stereotypes within two radically different societies.
None of the male or the female characters is accorded a mature, fully
sexed identity: all those who have a sexual life in the novel are depicted
as ultimately unfulfilled, yearning for freedom from the chains of their
fantasies—which are invariably displacements of desire. Zett Zobeida
and Oum Kalsoum may aid Idriss in his quest for bonding with his
native culture, but the novel uses repetition of epithets to conflate them
into one figure which functions as an incarnation of Islam. To make of a
human being a pure, absolute sign is, of course, to deny the very
relativity that is the condition of 'la condition humaine'. While Idriss
has not yet learned this truth at the end of the novel, the text's
configurations have alerted the reader to the fact that in modern Europe
neither women nor immigrants have the possibility of affirming the
purity and disinterestedness of the sign. And, more importantly, the
text's consistent play with analogies and contradictions suggests, against
its surface intention, that we should beware of believing whole-
heartedly in the Islamic sign as a sure antidote to the poisons of the
Western obsession with images and image-making, for the sign will
always mean more than itself, since to learn to speak and to read
involves the acquisition of the presupposition that meaning is
everywhere and in everything.

Idriss is not just a fictional immigrant; he is a trope, a figure of the
reader—who is herself or himself (initially, temporarily) constructed
by the text and in thrall to it. As readers, we are always 'immigrants',
transgressors into a domain which is neither wholly foreign nor wholly
familiar. Consequently, we need to liberate ourselves not only from our
own preconceived ideas but also from the 'tyranny' of the narrative.
While Tournier's novel may on one level seem to seek to impose
authority through narrative interventions, its self-referentiality
questions that very authority—for the text's manoeuvrings ensure that
the reader is shaken out of passive reception into hermeneutic

speculation and a rethinking of the value of memory. Writer-theorists such as Barthes and Borges have insisted that we read in a circular or labyrinthine way, constantly bringing into play our personal knowledge both of the individual text and of the library that we all carry with us. Tournier makes clear in *Le Vol du vampire* and in 'La Condition du romancier', that he now firmly believes in the co-creativity of the reader—who will always bring to his or her reading both personal experience and a degree of suspicion.

On one level, *La Goutte d'or* urges us to be credulous; on another, it warns us against reading naïvely, that is to say with an over-eager desire to identify with any of the protagonists. Sigisbert de Beaufond is inscribed in the novel as an anti-model for reading: he starts telling a story recounted to him by 'le colonel Alexandre Bernard' (**131**), and then goes on to identify so closely with him that, after narrating how Laperrine and Bernard slashed their wrists to drink their own blood in an attempt at suicide, he holds out his own wrists to show the scars (**134**). Idriss sees nothing, of course, because Sigisbert is a bad reader who does not know the difference between fiction and reality, as is evidenced by his slippage from 'ils' to 'nous'. In his 'Post-scriptum', Tournier reveals that he himself actually saw these scars on Bernard's wrists, but he also insists that Sigisbert is a 'personnage inventé et de surcroît mythomane' (**221-2**). While no detail of Laperrine's fate is false or even exaggerated, the ironic transfer of narrating authority to Sigisbert entails a repositioning of the text/reader relationship.

As we read through the novel, we learn more than does any individual character. Idriss's passage towards the threshold of adulthood is undoubtedly a powerful and persuasive narrative; the novel as a whole has, however, a pedagogic rather than a dogmatic aim, seeking to liberate the reader in a way in which Idriss cannot be liberated.

Chapter Four

The games writers play

A member of the Académie Goncourt, Tournier shares with his fellow academicians an admiration for the nineteenth-century realist novel, and in essays, interviews and visits to schools he repeatedly reaffirms his belief in the need for all novelists to engage in substantial documentation before beginning to write—indeed, he often says, self-mockingly and somewhat disingenuously, that he has little imagination and relies for his ideas and images on his various researches. His main models in this respect are Flaubert and Zola. Like them, he reads widely and voraciously; he also commits himself to personal investigation. He reiterates his admiration for Zola in one of his recent texts: 'de tous les romanciers Zola est certainement celui qui le plus consciencieusement "allait au charbon", et au double sens du mot quand il préparait *Germinal,* le roman des mines de charbon du nord de la France'.[1]

As part of his preparations for *La Goutte d'or,* he too left his library to learn from first-hand experience. For instance, in order to discover how North Africans are treated in France, he visited several foyers for immigrants, spent a day in the Renault factory in Paris, attended many Arab political and cultural meetings and even spent an entire night in a police van silently recording how the police dealt with Arabs without identity papers or a valid work permit; he spent a morning in an abattoir and an afternoon in a factory learning all the details of how polyethylene or PVC dummies are made (although, when he asked if he might submit to the casting *couche* himself, the technicians declined on the grounds that at his age it was medically inadvisable!); he spent several days with the calligrapher Hassan Massoudy, not only assimilating the theory of calligraphy but also learning how to manipulate the reed pen.

La Goutte d'or contains many pages presenting the information he

---

[1] Michel Tournier, 'La Condition de romancier', in *Vendredi ou les limbes du Pacifique, Le Roi des Aulnes, Les Météores* (1989), p. xi. 'Aller au charbon' is given in the *Trésor de la langue française* as 'exercer un métier régulier', which is indeed true of Zola's most consistent writing habits, but here it is to be understood as 'to get stuck in', an expression much favoured by Jacques Chirac. More importantly, Tournier is revelling in word-play, for when he uses 'aller au charbon' to denote Zola's project and methods, he is employing the trope of syllepsis (much rarer in French than in English) whereby the literal and the figurative senses of a word or expression are simultaneously evoked. See also p. **209**, where in the list of tropes supplied by Ibn al Houdaïda, syllepsis is defined as one of the 'figures de construction'.

gleaned from his reading and his investigations. In this respect, it is no different from his previous novels, all of which contain an abundance of scientific, medical, psychological, anthropological, historical and aesthetic information. Yet this novel was attacked more virulently than its predecessors by several critics, notably those who both disapprove of his 'traditionalism' and resent his success. The most obvious example is Angelo Rinaldi, who wrote an review-article on *La Goutte d'or,* maliciously entitled 'Connaissez-vous Pompignan?' (*L'Express,* 3 janvier 1986), in which he argued that Tournier had lost whatever inspiration he might previously have had and that he was now relying purely on his researches:

> Si complète et sérieuse qu'elle soit, la documentation n'est rien quand il n'existe pas de sensibilité pour l'irriguer, d'imagination pour la transfigurer, de style pour la rendre mémorable.

The assault was, and was meant to be, venomous. More worryingly, though, its conclusion is the result of a wilful misunderstanding of what Tournier is doing in his novel. He inserts only such information as is useful either for the narrative drive or for his metafictional designs— and he precisely plays with the different registers of his sources in order to catalyse the reader's active intervention. However, never does he believe (or write as if he believed) that documentary evidence in itself is, as Derrida would say, always-already appropriate in a novel: all depends on its contextual placing. For *Germinal,* Zola deliberately massaged the data he had assiduously amassed; for *Madame Bovary* and *L'Éducation sentimentale* (even for *Trois contes*), Flaubert manipulated his research findings selectively in order to use only what could serve his ironic narrative purpose; and for *La Goutte d'or,* Tournier carefully sifted through all his notes in order to choose only the information that would fit the scheme of his novel.

It is, of course, possible to view the compulsion to research as pathological and as revelatory of a desire to control or to alter fact through fiction, but Tournier's attitude to the use of documentation is similar to that of Zola, who, in a letter about *Germinal* considered crucial to the poetics of Naturalism (to Henry Céard, 22 March 1885), wrote:

> J'ai l'hypertrophie du détail vrai, le saut dans les étoiles sur le tremplin de l'observation exacte. La vérité monte d'un coup d'aile jusqu'au symbole.

Tournier is equally obsessive in his desire to acquire encyclopedic knowledge before he starts writing his novels, yet he too believes that reality can be perceived as truth only through a process of symbolisation or figuration. For him, meaning is to be found through interpretation, and it can then be communicated to others through parabolic texts which demand the active intervention of the reader.[2]

Already in *Vendredi,* in which Robinson Crusoe functions as the alter ego of Western capitalist man (and, indeed, of the novelist himself before he studied with Lévi-Strauss at the Musée de l'Homme), Tournier indicates that the compulsion to catalogue can never be anything other than an attempted defence against chaos. Robinson records in his *Log-book:*

> Je veux, j'exige que tout autour de moi soit dorénavant mesuré, prouvé, certifié, mathémathique, rationnel. [...] Je voudrais que chaque plante fût étiquetée, chaque oiseau bagué, chaque mammifère marqué au feu. Je n'aurai de cesse que cette île opaque, impénétrable, pleine de sourdes fermentations et de remous maléfiques, ne soit métamorphosée en une construction abstraite, transparente, intelligible jusqu'à l'os. (*V,* 67)

This belief in control-through-cataloguing is systematically undermined as the novel progresses towards its conclusion, which asserts that valid identity can be established only through a transcendence of European categories of knowledge and through a recuperation of childlike spontaneity. Facts are certainly important, but they must be incorporated into one's being (or one's text) through a process of assimilation or digestion by which they are in some way altered. Tournier gives the following definition: 'Éducation = initiation + information' (*VP,* 57), thereby making clear that for him mere knowledge is insufficient.

In the last chapter, I argued that *La Goutte d'or* is a novel which both describes how Idriss (mis)reads modern Western culture and engages its readers in a creative re-evaluation of their own positions as readers. It is also a novel which meditates on the nature and value of writing.[3] Tournier has written many short texts on the importance of writing by hand and not on a typewriter or a word processor, with a fountain pen and not a biro, and on the worth of writing at a lectern-desk (see 'Écrire debout', in *Le médianoche amoureux*). This commitment to the importance of the body in the act of writing is most forcefully expressed in the chapters on calligraphy in *La Goutte d'or*—and it is interesting that, when his works first began to be published in Braille, he devoted many articles and interviews to the 'superiority' of blind readers who use their fingers in reading and are

---

[2] See the definition of parabolic texts given in Michael Worton, 'Écrire et ré-écrire: le projet de Tournier', *Sud,* XVI, 61 (1986), pp. 52-69.

[3] In *Michel Tournier: Philosophy and Fiction* (Oxford: Clarendon Press, 1988), Colin Davis goes so far as to say that 'Above all else [...], *La Goutte d'or* is a novel about writing' (p. 164). I agree that writing is an important concern of the novel, but.in general I prefer to put the emphasis on reading, since, as Tournier and many contemporary theorists have insisted, reading precedes and determines writing—and Idriss's adventures consist of 'failed' readings which help the reader to read in a better and more creative way.

therefore in a closer bodily contact with the text's characters than sighted readers, who merely scan the page with their eyes.

Revelling as usual in etymology, he frequently insists that texts are *manu*-factured, yet he equally often insists that one cannot write a text unless one has a history as a reader. In other words, the bodily activity of drawing characters on a page alerts us to our physical individuality, whereas the act of thinking and remembering reunites us with our cultural past. Tournier makes no secret of the fact that his admiration for the works of his favoured literary precursors is tinged with jealousy and a wish that he had written them himself. He recognises that, like all writers, he is 'late-come' as Harold Bloom would say: all he can do is refer in his novels to the literary past 'avec un clin d'œil à l'intention du lecteur assez attentif ou lettré pour comprendre' (see *VP*, 54-6), thereby establishing a relationship of playful complicity with certain initiated readers—as will be seen later, when we consider his use of proper names. Tournier's response to his acute awareness of literary influence is ambivalent. He feels both an almost angry envy and genuine loving gratitude, but over the years he has refined a strategy of countering his resentment by inscribing into his novels quotations or allusions which function as signs of sameness, of affinity, and not as signs of difference, of a desire to impose a sense of his own originality:

> Peut-être le comble de l'art consiste-t-il à créer du nouveau en lui prêtant un air de déjà vu qui rassure et lui donne un retentissement lointain dans le passé du lecteur. (*VP*, 205)

Another, somewhat differently focused articulation of this point is made when Tournier compares his project to that of a prestigious forerunner:

> André Gide a dit qu'il n'écrivait pas pour être lu mais pour être relu. Il voulait dire par là qu'il entendait être lu au moins deux fois. J'écris moi aussi pour être relu, mais, moins exigeant que Gide, je ne demande qu'une seule lecture. Mes livres doivent être reconnus—relus—dès la première lecture. (*VP*, 189)

In *La Goutte d'or*, the anxiety of influence plays a crucial role in our perception of Idriss's progress. He accepts other people's views and stories, and even if he is occasionally perplexed by their obsessive self-mystification (as with Lala Ramirez and Sigisbert de Beaufond), he receives their influence passively, because he has no story of his own to offer as a substitute. The reader does, though—as does the novelist, who is much more concerned in this novel with the ways in which he can play with rewriting as a strategy of self-affirming recuperation. Much Tournier criticism still focuses on his use of myth, whereas we should now perhaps consider more urgently the metaliterary qualities of his work.

More patently than his early novels, *La Goutte d'or* shows that how one narrates is just as important as what one narrates. Those hostile critics who proclaimed that he had lost his way committed the double error of not recognising that Tournier has always striven to be subversive from within the walls of tradition and of being blind or deaf to his many statements which reveal his increasing fascination with the reading/writing and the writer/reader relationships. For him, writers can write only once they have read extensively, and they must then trust their readers to engage in a supplementary activity of creation.

While it is impossible, and indeed inappropriate to catalogue here all the texts he read as informational and inspirational background, I would argue that what is essential is that in his novel he 'mixed and matched' a wide variety of discourses, privileging none but rather according the novel a kaleidoscopic feel that makes us question (but not necessarily deny!) the authority of both narrator and novelist. If I use the metaphor of the kaleidoscope, it is partly because the novel treats of the problem of the image, yet I could equally well use the metaphor of the fugue with its insistence on counterpoint and on the characteristics and technical possibilities of the different instruments involved. (It is worth remembering that Tournier constantly reiterates his admiration for Bach's *Art of the Fugue,* which is, in his opinion, the summit of musical achievement and the best theoretical model for any artist interested in form.)

Amongst all of Tournier's research materials for the Saharan episodes of his novel, none is more important than Dominique Champault's extraordinary study, *Tabelbala.*[4] A book which Tournier continues to re-read, it is a mine of anthropological information which furnished him with all the exact details of daily oasis life that he needed. However, Tournier read this book as a literary text as well as a source-book: he rarely quotes Champault directly, usually rewriting or embroidering her phrases or carefully choosing one out of several words she uses for the same custom. For example, she first speaks of 'les enfants voués aux nègres' (Champault, p. 185) and only much later uses the term 'les enfants vendus aux nègres' (*ibid.,* p. 389). Given Tournier's preoccupation with the role of money both in erotic encounters (the Marseille prostitute; Achille Mage and *le grand Zob*'s 'cheptel' of rent-boys; the peep-show) and in French society's exploitative attitude towards immigrants, it is hardly surprising that he selected the latter term. Yet this choice also reveals that he is just as interested in the language employed to describe a custom as in the custom itself. One might thus go so far as to suggest that for him all texts are potentially literary.

[4] Francine Dominique Champault, *Une oasis du Sahara nord-occidental: Tabelbala* (Paris: Éditions du Centre National de la Recherche Scientifique, 1969). Page references are given in the text, preceded by the name Champault.

Another precious source was *Sans frontière: bimensuel pour un hebdo de l'immigration.* Tournier has subscribed to this from its first number (20 November 1979) and took notes from almost all numbers until no. 73 (April 1983). Many of these notes were not ultimately incorporated into the novel, serving essentially as a means of immersing himself in the atmosphere of the North African immigrant community. However, he read this magazine as strategically as he read Champault's study, occasionally seizing on individual words in reports: after reading a report of the strike by immigrant Metro cleaners (in *Sans frontière,* no. 12 [22 avril 1980], p. 6), he recorded in his working notebook 'Un gréviste accueille E. Maire et lui offre en dansant un bouquet de roses rouges'. While the local political implications of the strike certainly interested him, he was clearly attracted by the connotations of dance as a defining element of Arab culture and as a transgression of French protocol.

A third important source of insights into Arab culture was the *Journal de Mohamed,* a book that charts one immigrant's responses to life in France and to the family he left behind in North Africa.[5] Many of Mohamed's autobiographical statements focus on how much he is earning and on how he will share his savings between his wife and his father (see, for example, p. 121) and it is precisely these passages that Tournier annotated and glossed in his working notebook—more for their level of discourse than for the information they communicate.

These source-documents need not, of course, be consulted by readers of *La Goutte d'or.* Nonetheless, we realise that the novel is conceived as a *cento,* as a composition formed by juxtaposing fragments from other authors. In this we are guided by Tournier's revelation in the 'Post-scriptum':

> L'évocation de Sigisbert de Beaufond—personnage inventé et de surcroît mythomane puisqu'il s'identifie à Alexandre Bernard—est calqué sur le récit de ce dernier dont j'ai conservé l'enregistrement. Il en résulte que tous les détails rapportés sont authentiques... [...] Ces cicatrices, je les ai vues sur les poignets de Bernard. **(221-2)**

Tournier not only interviewed Bernard 'dans la ferme bressane où il a terminé sa vie' **(131)**; with Bernard's permission, he gave verbatim to his character Sigisbert many of the statements the Colonel made to him. So when the reader has finished her or his heuristic, linear reading which must include the 'Post-scriptum', s/he begins a hermeneutic, interpretative reading with the knowledge that (a) Tournier has been scrupulous in getting his facts right; (b) Sigisbert is, as a compulsive

---

[5] Mohamed, *Journal de Mohamed: Un Algérien en France parmi huit cent mille autres: propos recueillis par Maurice Catani* (Paris: Stock, collection 'Témoigner', 1973). Interested Anglo-Saxon readers will find an accessible source of similar documents in Alec Hargreaves's *Immigration in Post-War France: A Documentary Anthology* (London: Methuen, 1987).

storyteller or a *mythomane,* a figure of the author; and (c) every reader is drawn to fill in narrative gaps and to flesh out characters in order to make the novel work for them personally. As we shall see later, Tournier plays even more mischievously with the fictional possibilities of self-inscription into his text; for the moment, suffice it to say that the reader is alerted to the necessity to question both the originality and the coherence of the authorial and narratorial voices.

Several critics are today exercised by what they see as Tournier's didacticism, notably in *La Goutte d'or.* Their main objection is that he attempts to control his readers through the paratext of his footnotes and post-script which provide dates, sources and explanations of what is happening narratively in his novel. They see the paratext as a means of justifying a political argument which is partial and suspect. But this approach is mistaken, for it fails to take account of the nature of the novel—and, indeed, of the way in which it presents itself.

La Goutte d'or is a patchwork, not through lack of imagination but because its main purpose is to make its readers reconsider the agonistic relation between fact and fiction, between politics and morality, between one discourse and another. Like such contemporary British novelists as Anthony Burgess and A.S. Byatt, Tournier is an avid reader of dictionaries and encyclopedias and, like them, he studs his novels with etymological and informational gambits. He sees the novel metaphorically as a chess-board, as a game in which pieces can constantly change their value—but this game is a serious one, in which author, narrator and reader are engaged in an eternal endgame.

The paratextual use of epigraphs, footnotes and bibliographical details does usually signal an authorial quest for authority, but in *La Goutte d'or* these interventions are employed to fracture authority. In his numerous interviews after its publication, Tournier disingenuously claimed that it was his best novel because it was his simplest. Few readers would agree that its 'simplicity' makes it his best novel, but another statement he repeatedly made in 1985 and 1986 is intriguingly and complexly valid: 'j'ai enfin appris à écrire'. By this he meant not that he had finally found 'his' voice but that he had come to understand that any text written by any one person will be a rewriting of previous texts and that one should consequently incorporate other voices in order to allow the text to be the site of exploration and co-creativity by the reader. Only then will it be a 'true' text in the sense he elaborates in *Le Vol du vampire.*

The didacticism of which he is often accused is in fact subverted by the contextual placing of 'his' explanations. Consider the following:

> Tout le monde avait fui en emmenant chevaux, dromadaires, singes et sloughis, ces fins lévriers du désert qui posent leur tête fuselée sur les genoux des seigneurs d'Afrique blanche. (**33**)

This might initially be read as an example of the author intervening with superior knowledge to explain a term to a reader unfamiliar with North African culture, the explanation is not given by the narrator but by 'Abdullah Fehr, le conteur noir venu des confins du Soudan et du Tibesti' (**31**) who tells the story of 'Barberousse ou Le portrait du roi'. An outsider, a *Noir,* thus explains to inhabitants of 'l'Afrique blanche' the specificity of dogs which is part of their cultural heritage and indeed of their present. The implications of this technique are vast: who knows what? does any one of us understand our own culture? can truth as fact be imparted only through fiction? The point is not that we may not know what a *sloughi* is, since we have merely to look it up in a dictionary or an encyclopedia; rather, we must as readers question all established learning processes—which is precisely what Idriss does not do.

Tournier undoubtedly does intervene as author into his narrator's text by means of his footnotes, but these interventions are themselves by no means innocent. Before catching the car ferry for Marseille, Idriss goes to the 'bureau de l'O.N.A.M.O.' to obtain his passport. Tournier explains in a footnote: 'Jusqu'en 1973, L'Office national algérien de la main-d'œuvre (O.N.A.M.O.) acheminait chaque année en moyenne trente mille travailleurs algériens en France' (**94**). The naïve reader is grateful for this information, but other details such as the construction of an underground car park in the place Vendôme situate the novel well after 1973—when Idriss would not have been able to immigrate so easily. In an interview for *Le Gai Pied* (25 janvier 1986), Tournier stated: 'Les anachronismes dans ce roman sont pleinement pensés et acceptés'. This is no mere defence against any 'mistakes' he might have made inadvertently: it is an affirmation of his poetics of the novel which demands that readers perceive fictionality behind and within topical and authoritative references. Once reality is fictionalised, it may, as Sartre said when privileging theatre over cinema, become truth, but readers must initially 'play along' in order later to instal themselves simultaneously as judges and originators of the novel.

One further, if somewhat different, example of Tournier's play with extratextual references is to be found in the chapter on calligraphy where 'le maître Abd Al Ghafari' is a scarcely veiled fictional version of Hassan Massoudy, to whose *Calligraphie arabe vivante* Tournier pays homage in the *Post-scriptum.* However, Tournier does not leave things there. He introduces Hassan Massoudy into the novel as a 'fictional' character: 'Idriss apprit par cœur cette page du maître Hassan Massoudy sur la solidarité du souffle et de l'écriture...' (**199**). The page that Idriss learns by heart is central to the narrative which is charting his progress towards awareness of his body as well as of his culture. It could easily have been invented by Tournier—who nonetheless chooses to include in

his novel a page actually written by Hassan Massoudy that was published
a few months later in *Hassan Massoudy calligraphe,* to which Tournier
wrote the preface.[6] A real document is thereby incorporated into a
fiction and so loses (or undergoes a change in) its authority; a living
artist and a major influence on Tournier during his writing of *La
Goutte d'or* is given an intratextual role equivalent to that of the
invented story-teller, Abdullah Fehr, and is then resurrected or
rehabilitated in the postscript. So what is authority? Where is authority?
Only—passingly, ephemerally, dangerously—in the text.

The intratextual and intertextual weavings and waverings of the
novel could justify describing it as postmodernist. Self-consciously
aware of its late-come status as a work of literature and implicated in
Tournier's desire to 'faire du nouveau', it has a full functional existence
only when individual readers bring their personal knowledge and even
prejudices to their reading—which will be not a decoding but a
recoding of the 'Tournier' text. In most translations, chapter numbers
have been added, thereby suggesting that the novel should be read in a
linear way, as a logical, causal progression. It is undoubtedly true that
the narrator intends us to make connections between Idriss's various
experiences and that Tournier plays with prophetic structures as he does
in all his previous novels, but the structure of *La Goutte d'or* is more
subversive of narrative authority. Whereas he previously made much
programmatic use of epigraphs and chapter titles, in this novel he gives
only one epigraph—from Thomas Jefferson: 'Tu es tellement ce que tu
parais que je n'entends pas ce que tu dis' (7). Most readers tend to
assume that this epigraph is placed as a comment on how the French
treat Idriss and all immmigrants—refusing to hear their individual
voices when they conform to the fantasy-model of Western post-
imperialist ideologies (and silencing them if they do not conform!).
However, the epigraph can be read creatively in another way. It is
another of Tournier's 'clins d'œil' to his readers, one which serves as a
warning not to accept the novel at face value, as a simple story.

Each section is short and full of powerful images. The temptation is
therefore to define the novel as a *telephotogram* which is communicating
a message briefly and in a coded way. A more appropriate way of
perceiving the novel might be as a collage or montage whose final
meaning will be established variously by different readers. As we have
seen (*supra,* p. 61), Tournier wants his novels to 'already read' on a
first reading. By this he meant then that he wanted his novels to have the
familiarity of myths. While the novels preceding *La Goutte d'or* are all
grounded in myths or legends of European culture, in this novel (in
which, as he says, he 'finally learned to write'), there is much less
rewriting of the cultural past as a means of communicating the eternity

---

[6] See *La Goutte d'or*, pp. **199-200** and Hassan Massoudy, *Hassan Massoudy calligraphe*, p. 46.

and universality of mythic structures. Rather, he refers only episodically and subversively to past texts and transfers greater creativity to the reader, who is made to interrogate the relationship between writing and reading. The whole issue of authority is therefore brought into question, as the reader, faced with a kaleidoscopic text, is made to realise that a valid reading must be a hermeneutic, retroactive one.

In this respect, the use of a paratext of footnotes and postscript is crucial, for these are neither inside the narration nor outside it. They are marginal, yet they also tell the reader that the information given in the narration is not enough and so they are central to the process of reading. Since *Vendredi,* Tournier has been consistently concerned with characters who are marginal to the society in which they find themselves. The narrative message of *La Goutte d'or* is that, as an immigrant worker, Idriss is not an outsider but a marginal figure who has no voice; the structure of the novel as a complex of narration, intertextual references and paratext indicates that we readers should beware of being blind to the necessity, even the centrality, of the marginal: we must attempt to hear his stifled voice and thereby inscribe ourselves in the text by 'writing' his responses to what he experiences, that is to say, by becoming ourselves part of the paratext. In other words, reading becomes a form of writing!

Tournier's play with the possibilities of textual combinations extends even to publishing, in *Petites Proses* (1986), 'Le Peintre et son modèle', which he describes as 'Un épisode inédit de *La Goutte d'or*' (*PP*, 155-67). Recounting Idriss's encounter with a painter, Charles Frédéric de l'Épéechevalier, this episode would have fitted easily into the novel as he decided to publish it. So why exclude it and then decide to publish it almost immediately in another book? A first answer may be that it contains a highly erudite etymological play on certain French, German and Latin words and on their importance for Sartrean philosophy and for Saint-John Perse's poetics, topics with which the Belbali shepherd Idriss could hardly be expected to be familiar! On the level of realism, it was consequently suspect, especially since Idriss responds to the painter's explanations in terms which are not consonant with the linguistic register he is accorded elsewhere: 'Ça grouille de significations' (*PP*, 165). These are good aesthetic reasons for omitting the episode from the final version of the novel, revealing Tournier's preoccupation with tonal coherence. Nonetheless, the fact that he decided to publish this *inédit* a few months after the novel appeared poses a further problem, in that the novelist begins the narration of the encounter between Idriss and the painter with a summary of the first third of the novel. This text is undoubtedly one of the best introductions to *La Goutte d'or* (or, at least, to its politico-cultural intentions) precisely because it explains to the reader. It was patently rewritten and manipulated—only the last pages (158-67) are to be found in the manuscript drafts of the novel—so we must ask whether Tournier suddenly became anxious about the capacity (or the willingness) of his readers to perceive in his novel an activising commentary on reading and writing as well as the story of a young immigrant's initiation into French society. Not every allusion is explicated, but he does make clear, for instance, that the camel episode must be seen in the context of the adverts which show 'la tête rigolarde du chameau des cigarettes Camel' (*PP*, 157). Certainly a joke against Western advertising techniques, this statement also directs the reader to a re-evaluation of the narrative force of the postcard Idriss receives from 'la femme de la Land-Rover', which depicts 'un âne décoré de pompons qui brayait à pleine gorge, la tête levée, le râtelier largement découvert' (**52**).

Even if we are encouraged to see this *inédit* text as a lesson in how to read the novel, we cannot but rebel against the elitism implicit in its footnote on Charles Frédéric de l'Épéechevalier: 'On reconnaîtra facilement Carl Fredrik Reuterswärd' (*PP*, 158). 'Facilement' for whom? Surely only for those relatively few people who have seen this Swedish painter's work in exhibitions or in books. Aggressive as I may seem on this point, I would argue that Tournier's play with proper names is paradoxically both exclusive and inclusive of the reader as an initiate: he alienates us through the textual presupposition that we all share his knowledge and insistently draws us (back) into the text by making us think about the place and worth of extratextual reference.

In *La Goutte d'or,* Tournier uses proper names in a more mischievously—and more seriously—subversive way than in 'Le Peintre et son modèle', where the reader is told what connections to make. As we have already seen, Idriss's own name has multiple and contradictory connotations (common North African name, King of Libya, name of a soda—and, as Tournier once reminded me, the name of a character in the *Satyricon,* Petronius's tale of sexual initiation); similarly, Oum Kalsoum's name signifies her symbolic role as standard-bearer for Islam. Many of the other names have an equally potent semantic force, but often in a hidden, even elitist way. There are obvious jokes such as the translation of the soft drink *Oasis* into *Palmeraie* and the designation of the homosexual pimp as 'le grand Zob' which in slang means 'big cock' (although most of the translators discreetly obliterate—or perhaps do even not see!—the joke and merely transpose the name: in the English translation, *The Golden Droplet,* for instance, Barbara Wright simply calls him Big Zob). Once one knows how fascinated Tournier is with etymology and onomastics, one cannot but scrutinise all names, especially in a text which is explicitly confronting us with language problems (and games). Zob's nickname is, of course, a French one, so his acceptance of it is a signal of his desire to be linguistically incorporated into French society in order to take his revenge on it. (The nickname 'Biglou' he gives Mage is another sign of how aware he is of the categorising possibilities of French slang).

The novel's ludic intratextual play certainly sets up a connection between *le grand Zob* and Zett Zobeida through their names and through their (very different, and indeed warring) roles in Idriss's progress towards individuation and some sort of mature sexuality. The black dancer Zett Zobeida is, perhaps even more than the blond tourist, the originator of Idriss's initiation (see p. **31**), and she is also his final fantasy-destination. Tournier's choice of name for her must thus be interrogated. In all his previous works, he has examined the interactions between beginnings and ends, between Alpha and Omega, between etiology and eschatology, so to have a character whose two initials are Z is scarcely innocent. She can be seen as a symbol of two ends in Idriss's life: the end of his youth and, much later, the end of his exile from his socio-cultural heritage. She therefore represents an existential beginning for him precisely because she helps him to end and so can be seen as a quintessential utopian figure in Tournier's cosmological view of the world. Her name can also be read—through Arabic—as meaning 'reject the white'.

These interpretations undoubtedly have a place both in Tournier's writerly intentions and in our readings, but in their 'cleverness' they neglect the novelist's most important joke: Zett Zobeida is a character whom he has borrowed from *The Arabian Nights!* In 'Haroun Al Rashid and the Lady', one of the stories told by Scheherazade, the Caliph marries Zett Zobeida and makes her his chief queen, but while almost all the other ladies are secluded in the harem, she is explicitly presented as being emancipated, for previously she was a merchant in command of her own fleet.[7] In most European translations of Scheherazade's tales, the 'Zett' is only occasionally used, since it is not a name but a title signifying aristocracy, so that she is usually called 'the Lady Zobeida', 'la Dame Zobeida', etc. An avid reader of *The Arabian Nights* in several versions and in several languages, Tournier is aware of the meaning of her name and title, but he chooses to alert us only glancingly to her transcultural and transfictional role, this when writing of Oum Kalsoum, Zett Zobeida's alter ego:

> Sur le «Rossignol du Delta», sur l'«Étoile de l'Orient», sur celle qu'on appelait tout simplement *à la fin* «*la Dame*» *(As Sett)*, Mohammed Amouzine, le petit tailleur du Caire était intarissable.(**192**; my emphasis)

---

[7] A convenient edition in which the section involving the tales of the three calenders, Zobeida, and her half-sister Amine can be consulted is volume I of *Les Mille et une Nuits*, tr. Galland (Paris: Garnier Frères, 1960), pp. 76-174; this includes the 'Histoire de Zobéide', pp. 155-65.

Like Zett Zobeida, Oum Kalsoum is a symbol more than a woman.
Furthermore, the fact that 'Sett' and 'Zett' are alternative
transliterations of the Arabic word for 'Lady' links them both with
Mary, mother of Jesus, who in the Catholic tradition is addressed as
'Our Lady'. The Virgin Mary and Oum Kalsoum are historical figures
whereas Zett Zobeida is purely fictional, yet all three are removed (by
men) from their specificity as women and transformed into a
reassuringly safe tripartite icon—as wife, Madonna and Vestal virgin
(cf. p. 192). Tournier's subtle presentation of the compulsion to
symbolise women in societies whose religion is male-based and
patriarchal but whose daily life is dependent on women and matriarchal
constitutes a significant intervention into current anthropological and
political debates: it is only 'à la fin' that the Arabs enamoured of Oum
Kalsoum as an image of their heritage passed from metaphorical
description to symbolic appellation!

Tournier's play with names must also be seen in the context of his
contestation of writing as a necessarily coherent practice, since the
explicit equation of Zett Zobeida with Oum Kalsoum and the implicit
equation of these women with Our Lady reveal a concern with the
relationship between truth and fiction. Who is more real for the reader:
the two women who existed in verifiable time but who have been
appropriated by male discourses and fantasies, or the woman invented
by (the already fictional) Scheherazade and appropriated by Tournier?
And indeed, were not *The Arabian Nights* written by a man or men—
who borrowed most of the stories from Persian books, but the Zobeida
story from an Arab book, and who wrote them down in Arabic? These
questions need to be posed, precisely because they cannot be answered.
Despite the interventions of footnotes and bibliographical references,
La Goutte d'or is Tournier's least didactic novel: he seeks here to blur
the boundaries between truth, reality and fiction and to encourage his
readers to read all names with suspicion.

Since Genesis, our culture has taught us the power of names both as
markers of individuality and as proofs of belonging to a group. This
means that when a novelist chooses a name for a character, this name is
as important for an understanding of what he or she is and means as any
description of physical or mental characteristics. All novelists realise
this, but Tournier is particularly concerned to give his characters names
which appear innocent yet also draw the hermeneutic reader into an
exploration of their complex resonances.The names so far examined
involve a transcultural play which is both scholarly and mischievously
jokey. Most readers will, however, probably not see the point of the
names, so this practice could be seen as elitist, the full meaning of the
names being available only to those who share Tournier's erudition.

The charge of elitism can be made even more forcefully with

another category of names in *La Goutte d'Or:* those which refer to Tournier's own friends. As I have already pointed out, Charles Frédéric de l'Épéechevalier in 'Le Peintre et son modèle' refers to a painter whom Tournier knows and on whom he has written, but there is a footnote in the text to help us to make (and question) the connections between fiction and reality. Despite its panoply of paratextual guides, the published novel precisely withholds this kind of information about most of the names. For instance, Étienne Milan is a fictional version of the photographer Bernard Faucon, on whose work Tournier has commented both in radio programmes and in catalogue prefaces. The ornithological link between the surnames 'Milan' (kite) and 'Faucon' (falcon) is evident—and the fact that Faucon actually has a flat-cum-studio in the rue de la Goutte d'Or gives further weight to the 'effet de réel', as Barthes calls it, of Tournier's transpositional, fictional use of a real photographer. Furthermore, each of Milan's descriptions of his photographs to Idriss refers to one of the images published in *Les Grandes Vacances,* Faucon's collection of *tableaux vivants.*[8]

In 'Barberousse ou Le Portrait du roi', the official court portraitist Ahmed ben Salem and the Scandinavian tapestry-artist Kerstine collaborate to provide the 'ancien pirate levantin' Kheir ed Dîn with an image of himself which is ultimately acceptable to him because it is a radical transformation of two-dimensional painting into the three-dimensional work of tapestry—which also includes a 'fourth dimension', that of smell: 'une tapisserie est destinée à être vue certes, mais aussi à être palpée, et encore à être humée' (46). The message of the story is clear: figuration through art can aid all those who have a negative self-image to find and assume their identity, as long as they recognise that they need the creative intervention of an objective eye. This aesthetico-philosophical position underpins many modern Western literary works which interrogate reader-text relationships, but in the case of *La Goutte d'or* the naming reference to the two artists who 'save' Barberousse through their art demands a more complex reading. Ahmed ben Salem and Kerstine are scarcely-veiled figures of Ali ben Salem and of his wife Kerstine ben Salem, artist-friends of Tournier, for whom he initially wrote the story. He wrote the story out of fraternal affection: it was initially intended to be a personal gift to his friends; it began as an outsider's attempt to express his gratitude to friends who had helped him to understand the signifying possibilities of images. The story must consequently be read through the prism of Tournier's own life as well as through that of Arab or Persian folklore.

Monsieur Mage is another example of Tournier's play with real, verifiable people. The name ironically evokes the Magi of *Gaspard,*

---

[8] See Bernard Faucon, *Les Grandes Vacances: mises en scène photographiques, 1976-1980* (Paris: Herrscher, 1980).

Melchior et Balthazar and *Les Rois mages* and, given Mage/Biglou's
ocular deficiency and the novel's attack on the Western obsession with
images, makes us wonder whether the name is not yet one more
interlinguistic textual game: Mage could be an amputated form of
Image—(I-)Mage, that is to say, an image separated from its
subjectivity. At one point, Mage boasts to Idriss: 'Je tutoie Yves
Montand, Jean Le Poulain et Mireille Mathieu. Je déjeune avec Marcel
Bluwal et Bernard Pivot' (**143**). There are several Parisian name-
dropping in-jokes here which presuppose an intimate knowledge of the
respective importance of the celebrities mentioned, although Idriss is
inevitably excluded from this self-congratulating sanctum—as are most
readers. Yet Mage goes on to say 'J'ai besoin de toi, tu m'entends? C'est
inespéré, non? [...] Pour vivre, nom de Dieu!' (**143**). Just as Mage needs
Idriss if he is to go on living, so the narration needs the reader if it is to
function properly. Naïvety is thus posited as desirable, as a blank slate
on which information can be written. We need not know everything in
order to read the text, but the references to real people suggest that we
might research and learn for ourselves in order to be better readers.
Mage is, in fact, based on one of the very people he mentions in his talk
with Idriss: Jean Le Poulain, the celebrated French actor and a former
Director of the Comédie Française—hence the joke involved in Mage
using the 'tu' form to Le Poulain.

Furthermore, one needs to know that Tournier wrote the film-script
of *La Goutte d'or* for Marcel Bluwal and that he is friendly with
Bernard Pivot, who produced and presented the highly successful book
programme *Apostrophes*. These jokes undoubtedly pose the problem of
elitism, in that only a few privileged readers have access to the
knowledge that makes them work and this knowledge is indeed
sometimes so autobiographical in nature that only Tournier's close
friends can see the point of the references. An explanation of, or at least
one partial response to, this elitism begins to be found when one reads
carefully the note appended to the quotations cited in 'La Reine blonde':

> *Note:* Ces vérités éternelles inscrites dans les lignes du visage ont été
> maintes fois exprimées au cours des siècles et des millénaires. Nous avons
> choisi de les recopier chez les écrivains suivants:
> 1. William Wordsworth.
> 2, 7, 11. Ibn Al Houdaïda.
> 3. Goethe.
> 4. Alain.
> 5. Paul Valéry.
> 6. Germaine de Staël.
> 8, 9, 10, 12, 13. Edward Reinroth. (**216**)

Throughout Tournier's other works, we find many references to
Goethe, Alain, Valéry and Madame de Staël, and a couple of references

to Wordsworth, all of whom were real writers and thinkers, but Ibn Al
Houdaïda and Edward Reinroth are to be found in no encyclopedia or
reference book. The reason is simple: the author of these 'truths' is no
other than Michel Tournier himself. Other authors (such as Stendhal in
Le Rouge et le Noir, for instance) have invented quotations and asigned
them to invented authors, and Tournier invented the name Ibn Al
Houdaïda to imbue the *conte* with a Persian authority and/or
authenticity. However, 'Edward Reinroth' is a different matter, for the
surname is a near-anagram of Tournier (the more so in that 'th' is an
archaic German variant of 't'),and Édouard is Tournier's second
Christian name! The discourse of the two *contes* is (and is intended to
be) different from that of the narrator of the novel. These embedded
narratives offer parabolic windows onto truth, whereas the narration
deals with problems of reality, but Tournier cannot resist the temptation
to inscribe himself, albeit in a veiled way, in the fabric of his novel.

An analogous example is to be found on the opening page of *Les
Météores,* whose first words give a precise date ('Le 25 septembre
1937'):

> À 17 h 19 un souffle d'ouest-sud-ouest découvrit le jupon de la vieille
> Henriette Puysoux [...], fit claquer le store du Café des Amis de Plancoët,
> rabattit brutalement l'un des volets de la maison du docteur Bottereau en
> bordure du bois de la Hunaudaie, tourna huit pages des *Météores* d'Aristote
> que lisait Michel Tournier sur la plage de Saint-Jacut... (*M*, 9)

Both of these examples are textual articulations of his commitment to
blurring the boundaries between 'reality' and 'fiction': once written into
one of 'his' texts, the author Michel Tournier is no more and no less
real than either Goethe or Idriss; he is simultaneously inside and outside
of the text; in other words, he has become a fiction for whom there is a
referent in the world of empirically verifiable reality but whose textual
function interrogates the power and primacy of reality.

Images are powerful insofar as they give the illusion of full presence
—which is necessarily absent from them. Illusion's relationship with
reality is consequently structured by lack. This might initially be seen as
a justification of Aristotle's somewhat negative concept of *mimesis* or
artistic imitation as a copy of a copy of a Platonic *eidos* or Idea.
Tournier's philosophical position, however, is radically modern, close
to Heidegger's notion of *mimesis* as a dialectical process in which the
binary opposition between reality and art is constantly being
deconstructed. I would never deny that *La Goutte d'or* is a powerful
political novel, but I would argue that its main force lies in its
exploration and presentation of formal issues. Like Idriss, the reader is
in an alienated position, always lacking all the appropriate knowledge;
like Idriss, the author tries to make sense of his own life as well as of

that of his protagonist by fictionalising (and this includes fictionalising himself); like Idriss, both reader and author can establish a sense of their being and identity only when they recognise that they (we) are essentially constructed by the society in which they (we) live. This complex refusal of the authority of the 'real' is what makes the novel such an important contemporary text, for we are led to speculate on how and why 'la société du spectacle' is able—and empowered—to construct us.

It is perhaps Tournier's recognition of the spectaculist nature of recent European culture that renders his novel so relevant—and so democratic. The references to verifiable sources are interwoven both with references to (almost) unlocatable sources and with fictional inventions, thereby demanding that the reader work at trying to establish where truth or reality lies. This patchwork aspect of the novel is democratic in the postmodernist sense, in its promotion of reference as always-already presupposed: we do not actually need to know exactly to what the novel is referring but we do need to realise that it is referring outside itself—to yet another text which will always remain no more than a text. Autobiographical inscription is therefore no more important when it is operated by 'Michel Tournier, author of *La Goutte d'or*' than when it is operated by the reader. We all bring to our readings our personal histories, so why over-privilege that of the author? Tournier's novel both presupposes the reader's lack of precise knowledge and information and encourages the reader to read personally. It thereby obliges us to ask whether we actually need to spend time in libraries researching his book or whether it can be read 'naïvely'. The only answer is that, as individual readers, we must read both with all our accrued cultural knowledge and with an acceptance that hidden within and behind the narrative are specific sources: like Idriss, we need to go on seeking for an origin that can never be wholly found. In this way, we become equal partners with the author whose inscription of himself into a fiction betrays a certain anxiety as well as an element of self-mocking self-consciousness.

No reading, of course, can ever be totally naïve, because to be able to read any text means that one has already read other texts (even when, as infants, we read our first story or book, we have already read the micro-texts of illustrated alphabet books). Steeped in European literature and sensitive to the signifying processes of many Asian, American and African literary works, Tournier undoubtedly writes essentially for a Francophile reader. While he always plays with a vast range of intertextual references, his creatively exploitative incorporation of the canon of French literature dominates all his novels —even *Vendredi,* which is a rewriting of Defoe's *Robinson Crusoe.* This is apparent in two ways in *La Goutte d'or*. First, we find several clearly-marked references to canonical French texts, as when Mage quotes to Idriss the opening page of *Le Petit Prince,* identifying Idriss with Saint-Exupéry's 'fairy-tale' hero: '... c'est ainsi qu'en pleine solitude, avec mon moteur cassé, j'ai vu arriver le Petit Prince des sables, toi Idriss' (**142**). The allusion to Saint-Exupéry's story is appropriate, even comforting, in the context of a novel which exposes and interrogates adult Europeans' desire to project their need for a fantasy-image of other-worldly innocence onto a young Berber. However, the very evocation of *Le Petit Prince* means that Saint-Exupéry is, rather like Tournier himself, slipped almost surreptitiously into the novel as the author of a multiplicity of other texts: once evoked, he must become also the writer of *Terre des hommes,* whose tale of aviation is an intertext for the *récit* of Sigisbert de Beaufond/Colonel Alexandre Bernard. Second, *La Goutte d'or* contains several unmarked quotations or allusions. These are not innocent, unconscious borrowings; rather, they have a crucial function for the French-educated reader. One example, again from Mage's mouth, should suffice. Trying to explain to Idriss his own loneliness, he says: 'Tu vois, [...] dehors tout n'est que crasse et puanteur, fange et souillure. On pousse ma porte: ici *tout est luxe et beauté, calme et volupté'* (**141**; my emphasis). Mage is (mis)quoting Baudelaire's 'L'Invitation au voyage', as is evidenced by his use of the 'tout n'est que' construction and of four of the terms in the poem's refrain

> Là, tout n'est qu'ordre et beauté,
> Luxe, calme et volupté.

Mage's play with Baudelaire's verse poem depends on the structural equivalence between different terms which are linked by the 'et' construction, but, significantly, it makes no mention of Baudelaire's problematic 'ordre'. Indeed, his oppositional discourse has been prepared, as Tournier is all too mischievously aware, by Baudelaire's own revised version in prose of his poem in *Le Spleen de Paris,* where there is more explicit insistence on dreams as mere fantasies—and where 'grasse' (cf Tournier's 'crasse'!) is repeatedly equated with positively connoted terms. The way in which Baudelaire's terms are cited suggests that Mage is remembering the *Fleurs du mal* version, but it also alerts readers to the intervention of an author who plays with intertexts in order to point up the writerly need to rewrite others' texts and to 'correct' one's own texts. Mage 'gets it wrong' in terms of literary accuracy; the narration 'gets it right', since it exposes how, when we all culturally-approved clichés to make our individual points, we say and do more than we intend.

Another example of Tournier's ambivalent attitude towards French culture, the intertextual game played with Mage and his discourse of seduction, is rendered even more interesting by the fact that when Baudelaire rewrote 'L'Invitation au voyage' in prose, he emphasised his subversive parody of Orientalism. The poet-narrator describes his 'vrai pays de Cocagne' (itself a contradiction in terms!) which is 'noyé dans les brumes de notre Nord' as 'l'Orient de l'Occident, la Chine de l'Europe'. In this Utopia 'tout est beau, riche, tranquille, honnête'—just as Idriss and his fellow-immigrants on the car-ferry imagine life to be in France. On a first reading, Mage's brief allusion to Baudelaire may appear to be a mere episodic example of the French compulsion to quote from France's literary heritage. However, its function is more complex, and reveals much about one of the central elements of Tournier's literary project. Yet one more of his 'clins d'œil', it sets in motion the work of intertextuality which enables readers to be co-creators of the texts they read. There is certainly an assumption of shared cultural knowledge, but this is less elitist than might seem, for the French educational system ensures that few readers (or, at least, book-buyers) can be unfamiliar with Baudelaire's poems. Mage's allusion to Baudelaire thus reminds us of what we already know; it also— insidiously and determinedly—reminds us of what we may have forgotten. We sense that the quotation is almost but not completely right and so we are sent to the original texts. And... we discover what is 'wrong', but are then inevitably caught in the net of Baudelaire's poetic discourse, which we must read to the end.

Consequently, we are faced with a paradox: Mage, whose sexual fantasies are Orientalist, refers to one of the most powerful challengers of the Romantic tradition of Orientalism. Mage is unaware of this slippage, and the narrator is equally blind to it. The author, however, knows what he is doing: he is sending his readers on a quest which, not unlike that of Idriss, will lead them outside the confines of a focusing on what they think they know.

For centuries, European writers have used the term 'the Orient' to designate North Africa as well as the Far and the Middle East. This Orientalism is usually less about a genuine, distinterested fascination with another culture than a means of restructuring and having authority over the 'Orient', especially over colonies.[9] In other words, Orientalism is, on one level, a form of racism, an attempt to impose through literature the primacy of western ideologies.

La Goutte d'or depends for much of its force on the two tales influenced by Persian and Arabic literature, yet it also contests this aspect of the tradition of French Orientalism. Although eighteenth-century texts such as Montesquieu's *Lettres persanes* or Diderot's *Les Bijoux indiscrets* articulate a veiled critique of French society and

---

[9] For an extensive survey of the subject, see Edward Said, *Orientalism* (London: Routledge and Kegan Paul, 1978).

morality, they are essentially ethnocentric and use Africa and Asia as screens onto which to project European fantasies of both sexual and social domination. In this sense, Tournier's novel is certainly the work of an Orientalist in that, despite his readings of anthropological surveys, his descriptions of life in North Africa are written from the point of view of someone preoccupied with the ways in which domination operates in a Judeo-Christian society rather than in an Islamic one. Even the early remarks about domestic life in Tabelbala are infused with a comparative intention: with its rehearsal of many of Tournier's recurring concerns such as the nomad/sedentary opposition and the social role of both the gaze and the image, the writing repeatedly makes European readers speculate on their personal experiences of their 'own' culture. Furthermore, Idriss as Candide, as young naïve hero, expects to find in France 'la Terre Promise' (**103**). This metaphor has enormous power for those brought up in a Judeo-Christian context: it is central, for example, to Zionism, and also informs many of the prayers and hymns of Catholics and Protestants alike. Yet it is not an essential part of Islamic teachings. Idriss and his fellow-immigrants are therefore presented textually as already subject to the laws of what is both a desired 'Promised Land' and an irrevocably alien culture. On the ferry, they see first advertising images of bliss ('Le bonheur') and then images of riots in the Latin Quarter. As if this were not sufficiently problematic, the text goes on to relate how, once the French coast was in sight, loudspeaker announcements described the Château d'If as the fortress in which had been imprisoned the Man in the Iron Mask (Louis XIV's twin brother), the Count of Monte Cristo and the Abbé Faria, 'personnages célèbres d'Alexandre Dumas' (**104**). 'Célèbres' for whom? Not for the immigrants, as the text continues: 'La foule des Maghrébins reçut ces informations avec tout le respect de l'incompréhension' (**104-105**). Tournier is fond of reminding us of the almost obsessive extent to which the French take pride in their national literary heritage, yet this undoubtedly admirable sociocultural attitude can also be a means of excluding others, even when they come to live in France.

However, while Idriss shares with the other immigrants an uncomprehending and therefore humble, subservient respect for the literary Pantheon of his host country, he also perceives French culture and society naïvely. This very naïvety at which we may initially smile is used powerfully in the novel as a strategy which permits the novelist to engage his European readers in an aggressive re-evaluation of the place of culture in their lives—and, ultimately, of their response which is often as uninformed as Idriss's, though with the difference that they at least know the names of the great French writers. Idriss's naïvety consequently becomes the vehicle for an ironic assault on Western values because (a) he is a non-intellectual with whose lack of knowledge we can all identify; (b) he is a comic figure and so is distanced from us; and (c) his misunderstandings challenge us to reconcile our own warring responses to the culture that forms and tyrannises us. He sees France 'badly', yet 'innocently', and so no reader can avoid the novelistic push to rethink the hegemonic authority of Europe. I do not mean by this that *La Goutte d'or* is narrowly anti-European; rather, I would suggest that Tournier's novel questions the uniqueness of any individual culture and urges us to read France through North Africa and Islam and vice versa, in order to achieve a greater understanding of the political power of discourses—and to challenge the hierarchies which differentiate between the so-called First, Second and Third Worlds.

The central problematic presented by *La Goutte d'or* is not simply one of intercultural politics, though; it is also one of subjective identity. In this respect, the two 'Oriental' tales are crucial, since they both evoke —and pose—the question of origins. Each of the eponymous figures is afflicted with hair colour that suggests they were conceived in forbidden conditions: the red-haired Barberousse when his mother was having her period and the Blonde Queen illegitimately and under the first ray of the rising sun. In their presention of socially marginalised figures, both tales question the authority of codes which condemn the innocent for the 'sins of their fathers'; both interrogate the tension between a sense of the weight of genetic origin and the need for a self-determined identity. In both cases, the power of the image and the desire of the gaze-as-response are repeatedly juxtaposed in order ultimately to justify art as the means by which we may be liberated from the tyranny of superstition and, in the case of 'La Reine blonde', from a narrowly genital sexuality. I am not sure whether I can agree with Tournier's utopian vision of art as salvation; I would, however, argue with him that art can be recuperative, in that it permits us as creators, models or receptors to find through the prism of the artistic text a new sense of our own, individual being—because art is always an articulation of primal and primary responses to the world; because it is always a distorting, subverting reflection of society; because it necessarily involves and demands an interrogation of our *Dasein,* of our being-in-the-world.

The two tales frame the novel, albeit from within. 'Barberousse' shows how we may find and assume ourselves existentially through the images that others make of us. 'La Reine blonde' offers an analogous theory, but from the standpoint of infatuated spectators/readers: through calligraphy, Riad learns how to read the portrait of the queen: as a palimpsest. However, the tale insists that this mode of reading is a form of writing. If the lines of the portrait can be separated into a multiplicity of calligraphic signs which have semantic meaning and which, when superimposed, recreate the portrait, writing is clearly privileged over painting. In this respect, Tournier is clearly opposed to those contemporary theories of painting which insist on its essence as pure event. For him, every painting can and must be read. Riad's triumph is that he learns to 'déchiffrer la signification de la reine blonde' (215); in other words, he learns that meaning is everywhere but also, significantly, that meaning can and must always be re-created. Tournier's own discovery of the potentiality of Arabic calligraphy under the tutelage of Hassan Massoudy taught him that any one idea or sentence can have several calligraphic signs (the novel gives only a verbal account of the process, but it is perhaps appropriate to point out that Hassan Massoudy showed the novelist an example of how a portrait could be decomposed into, and recomposed by, calligraphic signs).

However, the tale and the preceding analysis of calligraphy suggest an even more radical view. Reading as writing and writing as reading are activities in which we are given an infinity of possibilities: the meaning of any portrait is never single but is altered by the ways in which we decipher—and then reconstruct—it. As readers or spectators, we should not see ourselves as the passive victims of a fascination with what is given to us: we should constantly reconstruct our chosen textual object according to our contingent needs and desires, whilst also recognising that the object has some kind of authority. We must learn— and accept—to be co-creators. Therein lies the essential lesson of 'La Reine blonde'' which operates as a powerful counterweight to 'Barberousse', in which Kheir ed Dîn allows Kerstine's interpretative tapestry-portrait to be authoritative.

'Barberousse' and 'La Reine blonde' articulate in different ways a belief in the ultimate intelligibility of all individuals and works of art. They thereby reinforce the novel's ideology, but they also fracture its apparently seamless surface, in that they are written in a different discourse from most of the rest of the text.

In his essay 'Barbe-Bleue ou le secret du conte', Tournier quotes with approval Perrault's contention that *contes* contain 'des instructions cachées' (*VV*, 38). He goes on to contrast the *conte* with the fable and with the *nouvelle*, or realist short story:

> À mi-chemin de l'opacité brutale de la nouvelle et de la transparence cristalline de la fable, le conte—d'origine la fois orientale et populaire—se présente comme un milieu translucide, mais non transparent, comme une épaisseur glauque dans laquelle le lecteur voit se dessiner des figures qu'il ne parvient jamais à saisir tout à fait. [...] Le conte est une nouvelle hantée. (*VV*, 40)

> Le conte est-il un vestige archéologique, ou au contraire une nébuleuse où se cherche l'avenir? L'alternative est peut-être trop tranchée. Il n'est pas sûr qu'à ce niveau de profondeur le passé et le futur se distinguent aussi clairement l'un de l'autre. (*ibid.*, p. 43)

Tournier's fascination with the *conte* is such that it has become his preferred form of writing: indeed, he now describes himself as a 'conteur' rather than as a 'romancier', and in *Le Médianoche amoureux* makes it clear that the *conte* is recuperative and healing—unlike the *nouvelle,* which is destructive:

> Il leur [à Nadège et à Oudalle] semblait que les nouvelles, âprement réalistes, pessimistes, dissolvantes, contribuaient à les séparer et à ruiner leur couple, alors que les contes, savoureux, chaleureux, affables, travaillaient au contraire à les rapprocher. (*MA,* 47)

The reason for this fascination lies in the between-ness of the *conte,* which is neither transparent nor opaque, neither a mere echo from the past nor purely a straining towards the future. Both its thematic content and its discursive register distinguish it from the realism of the novel; hence the importance in *La Goutte d'or* of 'Barberousse' and 'La Reine blonde' which frame the story of Idriss's quest.

This framing is itself doubly subversive. The tales are told within the novel, marking the beginning and end of Idriss's quest for an identity through images but not those of the narration, and they fracture the surface of the novelistic discourse even more than such other 'alien' interventions as Sigisbert de Beaufond's story or Mage's quotation of Valéry's 'Palme' (**148**), precisely they have the power of an archaic discourse which, like Idriss, we assume we must believe. As the narration makes clear, Idriss's full initiation into his Saharan identity is interrupted by Abdullah Fehr's *conte* (**31**). This should perhaps lead us to admit that the two *contes* form a structural frame but also frame the novel in the sense that they 'set it up' for a crime of which it is innocent: its intention is not to be didactic or to lay down the law but to alert us to the seductions and dangers of partial and over-simple reading.

The two tales are undoubtedly important learning aids for Idriss, but, despite their Oriental aspect, they in fact legitimise the culture of the image which the novel is purportedly attacking—and to which Zett Zobeida is the symbolic antidote.[10] Consequently, it is vital to note that at crucial moments in his quest Idriss remembers the litany sung by the crowd to accompany her dance (**30**; **113**; **154**; **220**). This song was invented, not borrowed or paraphrased, by Tournier, so we may justifiably see it as a form of authorial guidance, as an indicator of how to read this kaleidoscopic text. The ties made by sound, sense and etymology are complex and profound, yet above all they remind us that meaning can be established by the secret magic of poetry, by the free play of signifiers which transports us beyond logic and prosaic denotation

---

[10] For a different perspective on Tournier's use of the *conte,* see Lynn Salkin Sbiroli's essay 'Learning and Unlearning: Tournier, Defoe, Voltaire', which examines Tournier's interaction with eighteenth-century philosophical fiction, in Michael Worton (ed.), *Michel Tournier* (London: Longmans, 1993).

into the realm of speculation (for instance, 'libellule'—'aile'—
'libelle'—'écrit'— ['liberté' and 'livre']).

In all his previous novels, Tournier played with the juxtaposition of
different discourses. *La Goutte d'or* does this too, but it distinguishes
itself from its predecessors precisely because the 'alien' or apparently
marginal interventions are used not to legitimise the authority of the
main narrative but to question the power of all linearity, be it in writing
or reading. In other words, it passes power to the reader.

Conclusion

The critical reception of *La Goutte d'or* in 1985-1986 was certainly violent and divided, yet most critics focused on its content, thereby revealing that they had read it as a 'mere' document rather than as a novel and so were responding to what they, in diverse and subjective ways, presumed to be Tournier's political position on immigration and on contemporary French culture. The novel undoubtedly contains a sustained assault on the ways in which immigrants are consistently demeaned and betrayed by their host country. It also articulates, albeit in a different and more subtle way, several of the major themes that haunt Tournier's previous novels.

Of these themes, perhaps the most important is that of initiation.[1] In *Le Vent Paraclet,* Tournier gives the following explanation of the processes involved:

> L'initiation d'un enfant se fait par un double mouvement: entrée dans la société—principalement des hommes—, éloignement du giron maternel. En somme, passage d'un état biologique à un statut social.(*VP*, 19)

The adolescent Idriss's quest can be seen as an initiatory one, notably in his discovery of the hostility of the world outside the maternal comfort of Tabelbala and Islamic culture. However, Idriss's story is used also to rehearse the permanent Tournierian obsession with the nomad / sedentary opposition which, grounded in the Biblical tale of Cain and Abel, is an equally central theme in all his novels, and informs the recent psychological distinction he has made between the 'primaire' and the 'secondaire'(*MI*, 179-83). As is the case for many other Tournierian heroes, Idriss's quest ends when he realises that it has been a 'progrès *à rebours*' (*RA*, 106) and that the destination he has been seeking is in fact his starting-point. To use a theological concept of which the novelist is fond, Idriss discovers that Alpha and Omega can be conjoined, that in his beginning lies his end, and vice versa. At first view, Idriss may therefore seem not to have learned much, but he is undoubtedly modified by his experience of inversion, which Tournier defines as follows:

> l'inversion maligne-bénigne, cette mystérieuse opération qui sans rien changer apparemment la nature d'une chose, d'un être, d'un acte retourne sa *valeur,* met du plus où il y avait du moins, et du moins où il y avait du plus. (*VP*, 125)

---

[1] See in this conncection Emmanuelle Laugery's '*La Goutte d'or* de Tournier. Un roman initiatique', *Recherches sur l'imaginaire,* XX (1990), 215-34.

In other words, Idriss does not so much rediscover his roots as redefine them (personally and socially), albeit on a naïve or unconscious level. He may well be 'sourd et aveugle' at the end of the novel, but the reader recognises that a change has occurred in him and that he can now embark on a new and different quest.

The importance of travel as part of the learning process is stressed in all of Tournier's novels, whether one willingly chooses, or is forced, to depart from one's home. From Genesis onwards, this has been an important theme in our culture, yet for Tournier it has real personal urgency: while he himself travels both far and frequently, he also loathes having to leave his own house. As we have seen, the paradox of this tension is expressed in the title of *Le Vagabond immobile*. For Tournier, we all contain the warring elements of the nomad and of the sedentary, and we should admit this struggle within us in order to proceed to a creative reconciliation of the differences within ourselves.

Tournier himself is driven to travel, yet drawn to stay at home. Like Zola, he engages in eivnronmental and field experience. If Zola was led to the farmlands of the Beauce (*La Terre*), through the killing fields of 1870 between Reims and Sedan (*La Débâcle*), and from Mantes to Paris on a locomotive footplate (*La Bête humaine*), Tournier was led to rediscover the Sahara and, more importantly, to discover the hidden 'underside', the 'belly' of Paris, in his case the twilight world of Arab immigrants rather than the long-gone Halles central market. However, like Flaubert, he also considered that documentary research in libraries and in his study was just as important. After all, research is itself an exercise in intellectual otherness, in *vagabondage*.

The catalyst for Idriss's nomadism is his fascination with his lost photograph. This obsession permits the novelist to communicate, in a translated form, his own anxieties about how and why he needs, exploits, and yet dreads the visual image. As he explicitly states in his introduction to *Le Tabor et le Sinaï*, Tournier is aware that the opposition he sets up in *La Goutte d'or* between the modern West as a civilisation of the image and Islam as a civilisation of the sign is too clear-cut, too violent, for there are still many signs in the West and, increasingly, many images in Islamic countries (see *TS*, 9-10).

However, Tournier was writing a novel, not a work of social anthropology, and so could exaggerate a little. Furthermore, his assault on the image is justified on both the political and the philosophical levels and functions as an important intervention into the current debates about modern Western society and its obsession with the image. Most social critics, and especially those in France, insist on the ways in which the image is used manipulatively by those in power to maintain and exploit their power. *La Goutte d'or* presents several examples of this manipulation, but its focus is somewhat different. While it certainly exposes the *seductive* power of the image, it directs us to a consideration of the *complicity* of the *receiver*—who may see and accept passively, because that is what we are trained (indoctrinated?) to do. Idriss is not 'just' a foreigner or an immigrant; he is a paradigm of our communal alienation from the systems which govern our lives; he is a model of how each of us is simultaneously within and without, betwixt and between.

On the narrative level, Idriss is an *exemplum*, a warning for us about the dangers of complicity with the tyranny of any and all image-based systems. Yet Idriss is also—and must be perceived as—a character in a novel which is not only about him. The construction of the novel with its various breaks in the narrative surface repeatedly reminds us that we are reading a fictional text, a tissue of lies and truths that we need to read with (creative and generous) suspicion. Of all the quotations from predecessors that Tournier regularly cites in his writings, in his interviews and in his talks, the one that recurs most frequently is Jean Cocteau's:

> Je suis un mensonge qui dit toujours la vérité.

Tournier conceives of the novelist's art as a mixture of research and invention, but he also insists that the novel 'finished' by an author must be offered to anonymous and unknown readers who will then truly finish it in their diverse ways and for themselves—and who will determine for themselves where truth lies.

This theoretical dependence on the reader is exemplified and enacted in *La Goutte d'or,* in which the linearity of the narration is deliberately interrupted by different voices and different styles. I would indeed argue that the patchwork aspect of the novel is not, as many critics have said, its main weakness, but its greatest strength—precisely because it foregrounds difference and the impossibility of using one register or point of view to communicate a message.

Several metaphors could be and have been used to describe the novel: patchwork, *cento,* collage, kaleidoscope. What is interesting is that we need to have recourse to metaphors in order to describe this work which simultaneously relies on the realist and didactic traditions and challenges those traditions. *La Goutte d'or* is superficially traditional, but once one begins to read it attentively, one realises that it is subversive on more than the political level: by *presenting* a variety of discourses (none of which is definitively privileged), it proclaims its own non-innocence as a work of literature. In a sense, this novel is doing more than telling us a story; it is asking us to question what we think a novel should be or do.

The story of Idriss and the photograph that he will never—and should never—find is a simple one. On the other hand, the novel which purports to tell this simple story is highly complex. It rewrites the main themes of Tournier's previous works and consistently refers us back to the continuum of texts which is our prison-house and our liberation. Above all, it reminds us that no writing can occur or exist without the presupposed presence of readers.

La Goutte d'or treats of many issues which are central to our everyday lives. Its lasting force will, though, ultimately come from its textual insistence that the power of the 'author' must be transferred to the reader—who is in Derridean terms 'always-already' a spectator and a speculator. Its political, anthropological and aesthetic messages will continue to upset those who believe in what our governors say. We readers should perhaps constantly remember that art gives us freedom—and that this freedom includes the right to judge, for ourselves and in our own ways, every work we read.

Glossary of terms

Âge (troisième) [75] — retirement.
altérée [18] — mad with thirst.
arabesque [202] — non-representational Arab design.
arbousier [9] — arbutus, strawberry-tree.
L'Atlantide [131] — Franco-German film (1932) dir. G.W. Pabst, from Pierre Benoît's novel.
autochtones [133] — native tribes.
autosuffisance [50] — self-sufficiency.

Babouche [27] — heelless slipper, sandal.
baldaquin [33] — canopy.
balthazar [109] — gutbuster meal.
La Bandera [130] — French film (1935), in which a legionnaire falls in love with N. African woman, Aïcha.
baraka [90] — divine fortune, good luck.
baraquer [10] — to kneel down (of camel, dromedary).
belbali, pl. belbala [23] — of Tabelbala.
beta [108] — cooked, spiced bran + semoule.
bicot [123] — North African (derogatory).
biglou [143] — squinty-eyed.
Bikbachi [193] — lieutenant-colonel, i.e. Gamal Abdel Nasser.
blatèrement [153] — camel's whinnying.
bled [89] — country, or one-eyed town, place.
boqueteau [13] — clump of trees.
bordj [128] — small fortress construction.
borie [179] — hive-shaped stone hut.
bosser [167] — to work (slang).
bouffer [125] — to eat (slang).
bougnoule [121] — North African (derogatory).
boulot [167] — work (slang).
bourek [128] — savoury filo pastry 'spring roll'.
brâme [17] — bellowing.
briks [128] — stuffed filo pasty, often containing an egg.
brûler [51] — to be 'getting warm'.
bstila [128] — pigeon/chicken and egg-stuffed pastry pie.
burnous [28] — hooded cloak.

C.A.P. [165] — school-leaving certificate
catiminis [36] — menstruation.
Chaamba [10] — local nomad tribe.
chakchouka [128] — sloppy ratatouille, with poached egg.

chaulé [29]	whitewashed.
chéchia [128]	skullcap.
cheptel [23; 140]	livestock, herd.
chorba [128]	*marga* vegetable broth with vermicelli.
chott [9]	salt lake.
compte-gouttes [119]	dropper, hence here, 'parsimoniously'.
conciliabule [31]	whispering group.
couffin [23]	palm-leaf basket, or carry-cot.
coup fourré [119]	dirty trick.
coupure [125]	banknote.
coussinets [153]	folds of flesh.
crachin [109]	drizzle.
crottes [121]	turds, droppings.
Débrouillard [126]	resourceful, 'streetwise'.
'dégraissage' [118]	round of redundancies (culinary metaphor).
dinar [75]	unit of Algerian currency.
djebel [98]	mountainous terrain (name of a trail bike).
djellaba [68]	woollen hooded cloak.
djenoun [9]	evil spirit living underground.
dolma [128]	meatball croquettes.
Échantillons [143]	samples.
écumer [32]	to rove the high seas as a pirate.
embrenné [21]	befouled.
erg/Erg [10; 73]	high dunes or mountain range of such.
étrons [49]	turds.
Fegagir [122]	irrigation channels (pl. of *foggara*).
fennec [12]	desert wildcat or fox.
Foucauld [131]	Missionary and martyr (1858-1916), killed by Touaregs at Tamanrasset (Hoggar).
fric [70]	money (slang).
Gerboise [12]	jerboa, desert rat.
glycine [74]	wisteria.
godemiché [164]	dildo.
gommier [11]	gum-tree (often used for eucalyptus).
gonzesse [167]	young woman (slang).
goupil [46]	fox.
gourbi [15]	house of modest dimensions.
gri-gri [102]	good luck charm.
guerba [135]	waterskin, gourd.
guenon [110]	female monkey.
gynécée [203]	harem.

Hammam [107]	Turkish baths.
henné [24]	henna.
hippophagique [153]	to do with horse butchery.
Inch Allah [67]	may Allah's will be done.
J'm'appelle Slimane [165]	Song by Renaud: 'Deuxième Génération'.
Kanoun [190]	brasier, open fire.
kifkif (bourricot) [129]	it's all one.
ksar [29]	fortified house, village. Ksar Chraïa is one of the 4 settlements making up Tabelbala.
Litron [155]	wino's litre bottle of *gros rouge*.
littoral [101]	coast.
lumachelle [27]	fire-marble, a hard stone forming the outer casing of the flour-mill (shaped something like a kettle barbecue).
Maghrébin [105]	North African—from where the sun sets.
maktfah [128]	more likely *mqatfa,* which is pasta.
mandat [57]	postal order.
marabout [128]	holy man.
mater [166]	to ogle (slang).
méchoui [128]	spit-roasted lamb.
médina [139]	old town.
méharistes [136]	dromedary corps.
melon [170]	North African (derogatory).
miam-miam [121]	onomatopoeic for 'yum, yum'.
moricaud [143]	swarthy person.
mouflon [76]	shaggy, wild sheep.
muezzin [73]	muezzin, who calls the faithful to prayer.
mythomane [66; 220]	compulsive liar or fabricator.
Navette [90]	commuting.
niquedouille [41]	jerk.
niquer [218]	to fuck (slang)—cf. *NTM / BTS* ('J'nique ta mère/'J'baise ta sœur') rap group.
Oasien [11]	oasis-dweller (*oasis* is feminine).
O.S. [118]	*ouvrier spécialisé,* i.e. unskilled worker.
oued [17]	river.
Oum Kalsoum	famous Egyptian singer (1904-1975); l'Olympia's highest-paid artiste (ref. *Quid*).
outre [77]	waterskin.

Paille courbée [107]	bent straw.
passe-montagne [168]	balaclava.
pataouet [115]	*pied-noir* French.
pied-noir [115]	white French colonial settler in Algeria.
plongeur [119]	dishwasher (human).
plot [137]	bumper on flipper machine.
porte-à-faux (en) [118]	badly timed.
presbyte [93]	long-sighted.
porte à porte [54]	door-to-door (here, shooting).
procès-verbal [71]	report, statement.
Qanoun [195]	stringed instrument.
queue ronde/pointue [20]	circumcised/uncircumcised penis.
Razzier [9]	to raid, pillage.
recru [190]	sick to the teeth.
reg [10; 141]	stony desert.
ringard [150]	played-out, boring.
Roumi [32]	Christian European.
ru [9; 122]	subsidiary irrigation channel.
Salât [99]	one of 5/6 Muslim prayer times: c. 16H30.
salicorne [10]	glasswort, marsh-samphire.
sanie [157]	infected pus.
Saoura [71]	river after which *département* is named.
scarabée [11]	scarab beetle.
scinque [70]	smooth, snakey sand lizard.
sédentarisation [66]	tendency to settle down.
seksou [128]	couscous.
semoule [123]	coarse-ground corn, or couscous grain.
sloughi [33]	greyhound.
sole [12]	hoof.
souk [205]	covered market.
suppléer [121]	replace, deputize.
Tacot [61]	old banger, crate.
tagine [128]	stew cooked in earthenware *tazin*.
taquet [220]	the beating on a board that recalls a bird.
tazou [129]	Belbali name for *tazin*- cooked couscous.
tôle ondulée [64]	corrugated iron.
Toubou [66]	nomadic desert tribe.
trinquer [55]	to clink glasses, or here, 'pay for it' (sl.)
Varan [9]	armoured Saharan lizard.
Youyou [29]	female ululation of joy.

Bibliography

Works by Michel Tournier

The dates given are of first publication in Paris, but references in the text are to the asterisked Gallimard 'Folio' editions, unless otherwise stated. Bracketed letters are the abbreviations by which they are referred to in the text. Page references to *La Goutte d'or* ('Folio', no. 1908, 1987) are given in **bold type.**

Vendredi ou les limbes du Pacifique [V]. Gallimard, 1967*.

Le Roi des aulnes [RA]. Gallimard, 1970*.

Les Météores [M]. Gallimard, 1975*.

Le Vent Paraclet [VP]. Gallimard, 1977*.

Le Coq de bruyère [CB]. Gallimard, 1978*.

Des clefs et des serrures: images et proses [CS]. Chêne/Hachette, 1979.

Gaspard, Melchior et Balthazar [GMB]. Gallimard, 1980*.

Le Vol du vampire: notes de lecture [VV]. Mercure de France, 1981. Edition used, Gallimard, coll. 'Idées', 1983.

Gilles & Jeanne [G & J]. Gallimard, 1983*.

Le Vagabond immobile, drawings by J.-M. Toubeau. Gallimard, 1984.

La Goutte d'or. Gallimard, 1985*.

Petites Proses [PP]. Gallimard, 1986*.

Le Tabor et le Sinaï: essais sur l'art contemporain [TS]. Belfond, 1988*.

Le Médianoche amoureux [MA]. Gallimard, 1989*.

Le Crépuscule des masques [CM]. Hoëbeke, 1992.

Le Miroir des idées: essai [MI]. Mercure de France, 1994.

Le Pied de la lettre: trois cents mots propres. Mercure de France, 1994.

Suggestions for further reading and viewing

The volume of critical material on Tournier is considerable. These are books and articles which are particularly relevant to *La Goutte d'or*.

Blain, Gérard — *Michel Tournier*. France, FR3 Vidéo-Livre, coll. 'Témoins', duration 52 minutes.

Bluwal, Marcel — *La Goutte d'or*. France, FR3 (most recent showing, 11 September 1990).

Boubat, Édouard & Tournier, Michel — *Miroirs*. Denoël, 1973.

Bouloumié, Arlette & Gandillac, Maurice de — *Images et signes de Michel Tournier. Actes du colloque du Centre Culturel International de Cerisy-la-Salle*. Gallimard, 1991.

Cloonan, William — 'Word, Image and Illusion in *La Goutte d'or*', *French Review*, LXII (1988-1989), 467-75.

Davis, Colin — *Michel Tournier: Philosophy and Fiction*. Oxford, Clarendon Press, 1988.

———— 'Michel Tournier between synthesis and scarcity', *French Studies*, XLII (July 1988), 320-31.

Jay, Salim — *Idriss, Michel Tournier et les autres*. Éditions de la Différence, 1986.

Merllié, Françoise — 'La Reine blonde: de Méduse à la muse ou comment les mots délivrent de l'image', *Sud*, XVIᵉ année, 61 (1986), 14-29.

———— *Michel Tournier*. Belfond, 1988.

Petit, Susan — *Michel Tournier's Metaphysical Fictions*. Amsterdam: John Benjamins, 1991.

Rosello, Mireille — '*La Goutte d'or:* le peep-show, la vitrine et le miroir sans tain', *Études françaises*, XXIV, 3 (Winter 1988-1989), 83-96.

———— *L'In-différence chez Michel Tournier*. José Corti, 1990.

Salkin Sbiroli, Lynn — 'Scrivere la fotografia: il ritratto dell'artista ne *La Goutte d'or* di Tournier', *Micromégas*, 35 (1986), 65-77.